BIG MAMA'S LITTLE BLACK JESUS

William Roosevelt Leggette

authorHOUSE®

AuthorHouse™
1663 Liberty Drive
Bloomington, IN 47403
www.authorhouse.com
Phone: 1-800-839-8640

Published by AuthorHouse   01/11/2012

ISBN: 978-1-4685-4282-0 (sc)
ISBN: 978-1-4685-4322-3 (e)

Library of Congress Control Number: 2012900724

Any people depicted in stock imagery provided by Thinkstock are models, and such images are being used for illustrative purposes only.
Certain stock imagery © Thinkstock.

This book is printed on acid-free paper.

Because of the dynamic nature of the Internet, any web addresses or links contained in this book may have changed since publication and may no longer be valid. The views expressed in this work are solely those of the author and do not necessarily reflect the views of the publisher, and the publisher hereby disclaims any responsibility for them.

CONTENTS

Pictures

ACKNOWLEDGEMENTS

Many, many thanks to all the many, many people that encouraged me to put my life story to pen and paper, to those people that believed in me; and to those who listened to the tapes and said, "That ought to be a book", "Do it!" Especially to Mom Charlotte Beamon who was the first that told me, "You should write a book, Brother Leggette."

Thanks to my Lord and Savior Jesus Christ for giving me the strength to go through the storms of life I experienced along the way and to reach this peaceful shore of old age.

To my sisters; Olivia who helped to proof-read the finished copy, encouraged and held me up when I didn't think it was going to happen soon enough and to Margie who encouraged me to think positively, that it would come to pass.

And with special thanks and honor to Ms. Poet Laureate herself, of New Jerusalem Church, Mrs. Alma Jones who wrote the introduction we put on the tapes for distribution. Also thanks in memoriam to her husband, Mr. John W. Jones (1937-2011) who allowed her to take the time to assist me in my endeavor.

A shout-out of "Thanks" to all the pastors mentioned in the book that encouraged me to reach for the "Him-possible" and who also permitted me to write of our encounters. I especially want to thank Pastor Tammy Gibson, who prayed for me and prophesied that for me, the best is yet to come.

To my family, my children and my grandchildren, my seed, here and to come; you have encouraged me in ways beyond description, because I am leaving these words for you to look back into the past and understand how and why I came to be in California; some of the things that happened to me before I got here and some of the storms of life I met, on my way to get where I am.

Thank you, Aaron (my brother-in-love) for your educator's view-point of my scribbling. To my youngest daughter Griselda, for the title you suggested; to my oldest daughter Gretchen, for putting up with my continual requests for going hither and yon to get the book into print. Thank you Grace for being here for me when you came home from the military. To my sons Grant and "Q", thank you for all you've done to promote the success of this endeavor.

Thank you Evangelist Ramona Davis for helping me to get that taping done.

And not least of all, to my wife Marie, thank you Sweetheart; for all the time you sacrificed on your computer to make it all become a reality. Without your support, this would still be just a pipe dream unchartered and a wish unconquered.

THE BIRTH AND SURVIVAL OF A MISSISSIPPI SHARECROPPER

I'd like to say, "Greetings to you in the name of our Lord and Savior Jesus Christ". This is yours truly, Little Brother Leggette. I'd like to put some of my life on this tape to let some of you all hear what happened to me and the way I was brought up living in the Deep South prejudice, but God brought me out. The name of this here testimony will be: "Roosevelt Leggette: Big Mama's Little Black Jesus, A Country Boy". My daughter helped me pick that name.

Brother William Roosevelt Leggette

I was born sixty-seven years ago to Jodie and Azalee Leggette. The Lord blessed me to be the second child of twelve. Seven boys and five girls and I was the second oldest. We had it hard. Coming on up through the years, late in the midnight hour I had to cry, not sometimes, a lot of times. My life was one of the most prayerful lives that ever was simply because I prayed day and night; every day asking the Lord to bless this big family. The women was dying by the score by child birth and I was one that was concerned about my mother. We had one lady in the neighborhood, her husband went to get the midwife and when he got back, it was so far he had to go, she was dead. So look like my mother was getting pregnant every year. So we farmed; we lived off of milk and bread, corn bread at that, molasses to be nice about it. We say syrup and fatback. Kill a hog and made our own bacon.

But, we had to walk to school, five and six miles and more. We walked in the rain, in the snow, in the sleet and in the ice. Sometimes, most of the times, when we get to the schoolhouse our fingers, ears and nose and toes were so cold we had to go out in the woods and get wood and make a fire. And we all would crowd around that old country heater and when our fingers start thawing up they start stinging like you sticking them with a pin but only a thousand times worse. So what we did was we stood there for a while and finally it stopped; the sting probably went out.

Sometimes it would rain all day while you was at school. We had to cross something, you call it a branch; a creek. That was a stream of water; out here we call it a river. We would go across in the morning, it would be nice and dry, but it would be raining when we would come back that evening. Oh my God! The water rained, it be raining all day and the water'd get up so high it'd cover the bridge. You couldn't see the bridge! What we did was about twenty five or thirty kids walking along the roadway, one kid would, (sometimes it would be me,) would get a stick and feel, we'd catch our . . . , everybody would catch hands, join hands just like you do prayer for church and then feel and see if the bridge was yet there. Sometimes the water woulda wash the bridge out. We would hold on to each other's hand and the lead person would feel and say, "Oh yes it's still here." We'd walk on cross and the water was so swift it was almost to sweep us in, but by holding to each other, that held us up. It could have swept the bridge away and washed us all down the river. But God! God blessed us to go across, all of us safe to go home and tell our mother's about it.

On our way to school the white people would pass us in the buses and holler out the window "Walk nigger, walk, that's what you supposed to do!" They would throw spitballs at us and try to spit on us. We couldn't retaliate. But if it was this day and time they would knock all the windows out with rocks and things but you couldn't do that back then.

I remember when we got home from school we had to do our homework, go out and get wood, get ready for the night, milk the cows and slop the hogs and do what we had to do and after we finish that I had to go to the white people's house. They came to my mother's house and told her to let me go every evening after school and work for them and they would give me clothes and shoes, to help the family. I'd go work after school; they would give me boxes of clothes, shoes, canned goods. I was thankful and I took it (pause) I took it home, the reason it was so touchy that time was I would take it home and my mother would share it with the family. When you take a box full of stuff like that home it doesn't matter how small it is or how large it is, somebody could wear it. I want you to know my friends, my dearly beloved that went on for years. That's the way we lived.

I remember my Dad was a sharecropper. That means we would farm the man's land, we called it working on havers. Whatever the crop was that year after we gathered it, you gather the crop and sell the cotton and we had to pay for our half of the fertilizer, our half of the seeds. Then we had to farm it all, gather it all, the white man didn't have to do nothing but sit back and take our money. The bargain was I let you use my land; you farm it and give me half of everything you make. Whew!

So but the bad part about it, my dad never would come out of debt. Every year that the Lord sent we would get deeper and deeper in debt. That white man would sit down to the breakfast table, a table Dad made with his hands and tell us that "Sorry you didn't come out of debt this year".

Hear that song "I thank God for momma" well I thank God for Momma and Daddy. So my daddy got tired of that mess, he told my mother, he said, "I'm leaving here today". Mother told him she said, "You can't leave here 'cause we owe that man four, five hundred dollars or whatever it is" that was like a million now. Dad said, "I don't care I'm getting out of here". He took all his children and that little ole furniture that we had, ole wooden stove, ole homemade chairs, homemade beds, homemade benches; put everything we had in one wagon and moved us away from there by night, our dogs, our cats. But do you not know that next day that white man came and moved us all back on his place. My dad asked the man that we moved onto his place, he said, "Can he balance for many years that we was staying there, we did never come out of debt and he didn't have any money to pay. Moved us back and we stayed there I don't know how long.

Mother: Azalee Leggette   **Father: Jodie L. Leggette**

But there was a man that came out of Texas with a big cowboy hat; he had some undeveloped land. He told my daddy said, "If you would go and develop the land and work it, I'll buy you two mules, a wagon, some pliers, all the tools you need and the seeds and the fertilizer. All you have to do is pay me out of your crop gathering. You keep two bales of cotton all that money is yours and give me one. What you make off your two bales of cotton pay for what your fertilizer and seeds cost. The cost and whatever I'm charging you for the mules, pay a little bit on that". So that's the way we got out from under that mean taskmaster, out from under bondage.

So one day I was . . . , we was at home one night, we didn't have no electric lights, we was out in the woods with a lamplight. We heard such a beating about a block from my house. We heard a man groaning like an ox, my mother was crying, we didn't know whether it was a black man getting lynched or what, that's what we thought it was. But to our surprise there was a white man. Some lady, his girlfriend said, he raped her. The girl's father took that man, they was about fifteen of them, took him right there in front of our house and they lynched him. Beat him 'til he groaned like an ox. I guess they wanted to make it look like we did it I reckon. But for some reason he didn't die completely, he came to himself. And he saw that little lamp light that we had, he came to that light, knocked on the door, we was afraid to open the door 'cause we heard the beating.

But he told us who he was through the door, what happened and could somebody go get his dad. We knew him, we knew his dad, we was afraid to go get his dad but he was in such a condition. Look like he been through a meat grinder. So what we did was, my brother and I went through the woods and got his father. His father was a little ole justice of the peace. He came to the house he almost went crazy when he saw his son. My mother asked him and said, "Is something you could do about that isn't there?" He said "Well, not a whole lot I can do about this simply because what they have him for they could have put him in prison for life". So they went on and forgot about it.

MY FIRST CHRISTMAS MIRACLE

So I told you a few minutes ago that my life style was a hard one. Christmas was a very important time in our life. Glory to God! What we got for Christmas was not what you getting now, there was twelve of us. We got six apples, six oranges, nuts, grapes, peanuts, pecans all that kind of stuff. Little candies, little water guns, little paper air planes, something like that. My sisters got little tea sets, little dolls. It was seven boys and five girls so you know it was a rough life.

So this one particular Christmas we had a bad winter. And we had this white man, we thought white people had everything; we had a white man that lived not too far from us. You understand we would go to him and borrow money all through the year. And with this big family that we had we was glad they let us have money because we would go and work his farm. White people couldn't work a farm, no way, they would hire everything out. We'd go to his place and work his farm and we could produce a lot of work because of twelve kids' mother and dad.

So we go and borrow money from him and he would let us have it, no problem. This particular time Christmas fell on Sunday and Christmas Eve fell on Saturday. My mother told me to go to this man's house and tell him to loan her twenty dollars. Twenty dollars would buy a lot of stuff that day and time. It was like four hundred, five hundred dollars. I prayed all the way there to the man's house, mother caught a ride to the town, she knew I was gonna bring the money and was waiting on me.

I went and got to his house, I told him the story, "My mother gone to town and she told me to ask you to loan her twenty dollars, we'll come by and pay it back next week". He said "I don't have it". Tears start coming down my face, the man looked at me and I said "I don't know what we gon' do now, whole family; we don't have nothing for Christmas, she down there depending on me knowing you gon' have it". And I walked outta his back door. I had to go to the back door because you didn't go to white folks front door. I walked out that back door with tears in my eyes, Hiyah! Boy this is juicy I'm glad I'm putting it on tape with no pictures, 'cause I don't want you to see me now. That's why I'm putting this on tape with no pictures.

And I cried all the way home, when I got to almost home there was a little stream of water running down through the field and I got on my knees and washed my face so my sisters and brother wouldn't see the tear marks on my face and I straightened up and dried my face off on my shirt. And then I went on home. I got within a few short ways of the house, glory to God, can't hardly tell this one. Let me cut it off for a minute. (Pause in tape) Well I'm back now, had to go cry that one off.

When I got almost home I saw my brothers and sisters running outside they was excited they was rejoicing I felt so bad. I thought they was excited because I had the money and I knew I didn't have it. They figured they was gone get something for Christmas and I knew they wasn't but when I got almost to the house; you cain't guess what happened! You wouldn't hardly guess in a million years what happened! Yes! God had moved in a mysterious way, in such a miraculous way, (crying) in such a marvelous way. That man had came to my house, this may not seem like much to you all 'cause maybe you have everything that you ever wanted. But I had nothing! The man had came to my house and left the twenty dollars. That was what they was rejoicing about. I took the money, walked on out to the highway and caught a ride about eighteen or twenty miles to town and gave it to mother.

She went and bought our little ole Christmas. She'd get six apples, six oranges, some candies, some cakes, and what have you and in the middle of the floor she would put a little pile over here, that was my pile. A little water gun, a little paper airplane, a balloon or something like that and they would sit up half a night putting out stuff for all the children and we would get up and she would direct us to our pile and I found in my pile (crying) half a apple and a half a orange and a water gun and a airplane. And I was excited because of my Christmas. But there was one thing that I always wanted and I never did get it as long as I lived there with my mother and my dad, I was twenty one years old when I left. I wanted a red bicycle and I wanted a cap pistol, matter of fact I wanted two cap pistols one on each side so I could be like a cowboy. Young people ask, "Brother Leggette, why are you trying to put that on tape?" Simply because there are some people, some children getting everything they need, everything they want and they don't appreciate it. Even my kids getting the stuff that they want, that they need, maybe some of them don't appreciate it, my grandkids.

LAZARUS RISING: HARDSHIP, HATRED & HEALING

I want you to know that after Christmas was over, we would go back to our regular routine of life; that was working. I would go to town and get groceries, had to ride the mule for about ten miles.

I remember I went into this little ole town to three stores and I had to get the groceries and my mother gave me a note and I would charge it off, put it on the charge account. She would give me this note and I would go around and read it, get it, bring it to the counter and let them charge it. But this particular morning the man told me he said "Tell your dad I can't let him have nothing today." It was raining. But I chose this store because the next store I knew I could get it there but this man here was something else. When I go to his store I had to let him read the note. What happened is that I went there once and got my stuff and brought it up to the counter. My cousin told me he's an old man, the white folks said that I was a smart nigger, I wouldn't do like everybody else. I would go around and get my own stuff and bring it up there and put it on the charge account. Said they were gone to catch me in that store one day and beat my brains out. That's why I wasn't going to that store but I had to go and get it that day but I had no other choice.

And one day I went to get some groceries and I didn't go to the mean store because of the way they treat you. You know you don't want to go to a place where white folks talk to you crazy. I went to the store where the man talk to me nice. On my way back the guy saw me at the other store, He said "tell your dad that if he don't come pay me I'm gone send the Klu Klux after him. I said "oh my God" in my mind but out loud I said "What?" and he said, "Don't say "what" to me say "Sir". So I went on home but I came back to the store again. I had turned twenty-one years old and I was ready to get out of Mississippi. And I was a big boy. I thought I was proud that I was grown and there was a little girl at this particular store and she had just turned thirteen years old and her little boobs start showing and this white man said now I had to say, "Yes ma'am and no ma'am" to her cause she was getting to be a big girl now and she was growing up. I said yes ma'am and no ma'am to her for about a year.

First, I want to step back just a little bit and let you know some things that happened to me. God blessed me with a TV screen that follows me around everywhere I go. I see stuff happening and tell my wife and my kids now "it come to pass". I told my mother and all my sisters and my brothers "it come to pass". We live by that; it's a gift. A lot of you may not know what I'm talking about. I can look at you and tell you almost what you ate yesterday. I can tell what's going to happen tomorrow. If there's gone be a death I could tell you almost where it's gone be but I couldn't tell how long it's gone be. I never could measure the distance.

The Lord worked a miracle in my life. I had the eight-day pneumonia; my brother had had it first. I laid on my deathbed dying and I saw death when it came in the room that morning. I was spitting up cold blood by the mouth full, my lungs was full of blood.

So I told my mother and dad "y'all better do something quick I'm not gon' be here long". My mother said, "Pray son". I said, "Mother I prayed but God won't hear my prayer". She said, "Pray". I looked up into the ceiling, I hadn't repented, I hadn't done nothin', just a regular person, an ordinary person. I said, "Lord I heard the preacher preach about you, I heard the teachers teach about you and I hear the folk talk about you. I said "if there be a God up there, if you heal me I'll live for you the rest of my life". And my mother sent my brother to go get this man to take me to the doctor. He got on the mule and we got the man. The man had an ole raggedy truck and it had rained all day long, we had a September gale and it was raining all day. This was Christmas time but it was the worstest part of the year, the winter.

But the man came, he had to go about 10 or 12 miles to go to the doctor's office. It took him all day long to get ten miles. That truck kept drowning out and he had to get out his cloth and dry off the distributor. We finally made it to the doctor's office; the doctor looked at me and sent me from there to the hospital. It was about another four or five miles. This guy took me to the hospital and my mother asked the doctor at the hospital would I have to stay and he said "Yes ma'am this young man gonna have to stay 'cause we knew only one man who was in his condition and that man was only one degree lower than your son and he died".

There I was in the hospital. Christmas right around the corner, my birthday the twenty third of December. I want to be home with the family, unfortunately I was there in the hospital, they loaded me up with that medication. I didn't know I was in the hospital, when I woke up in the morning I was in a ward with nothing but white men. The way I was brought up was, a black man couldn't get nowhere near a white woman; couldn't even look at 'em. That's why Emmett Till when he whistled at the bird they thought he was whistling at the white woman and beat him to death, he was just a little kid. I woke up; I saw one white lady had one hand in my face on my forehead; one had one hand on my chest. They were praying for me. I woke up, Oh glory to God ! I thought it was judgment day and these white folks and I were the only one there. I don't want you all to take this testimony lightly. You talk about roots? I came up through that kind of condition. I woke up and thought it was judgment day, white folks looked at me like a bulldog. I was sitting up in my bed they was sitting up all around me looking at me. Then, I laid back down. They said" Let's let him go, he's tired, he don't feel good. We'll come back tomorrow." They told me they were gone come back tomorrow and sure enough they came back the next day and they prayed for me again. I was the youngest one there, in a few days I was out of that hospital. I was completely out of it. In fact I was walking around getting them ole mean looking white folks sodas out of machines, whatever, candy bars. I was one of the most, nicest persons you want to see because I know that God had something better for me.

DELIVERANCE FROM BONDAGE

We were living in a house right up the hill; under the hill from where my grand daddy was living. My first cousin went out and what he did was, he hit a white man in the mouth with a beer bottle. They was out drinking, you know how they do. So a mob came to the house that night for him. When that mob came after him, my grand daddy knew where he was; he was not too far from the house at one of his friend's house. They made him tell where it was but God worked another miracle! It was raining; it looks like all my stories are raining stories. It was raining, but first they searched the house, they searched the garage but couldn't find him. So they took off up the hill there to get him. We didn't have a telephone what we could call him.

So what happened was it started raining so hard, they couldn't go up that hill. My first cousin, my mother's oldest sister's oldest son, he walked through the woods, he was staying with my grand daddy. They told him what happened. They went out to the garage, he and his cousin. They both had a 410 shotgun apiece. They had 'em loaded; I don't know how many shells the thing would hold maybe seven or eight apiece. And they waited out there for this mob to come back by. The mob came back by, went into the house and searched the

14

house again; oh thank God they didn't go to the garage! If they had went to the garage they would have found him in the garage but they was standing there with a 410 shotgun apiece. So the people kept going, like my cousin said "I'm going to leave it in the hand of the Lord". We took him and we shipped him out by night, to Springfield Massachusetts. He got out of that one; we saved him. Raining, that's what saved him.

We went and farmed that next year we made enough cotton at another man's farm they cut our acres, but this man let us farm his land. We made a bale of cotton an acre, we made enough money and my mother took it and put it in the post office. I told my cousin I was coming to California this summer and look for me. He said he was coming back and had a seat for me but when he got back he gave my seat away. I went to the post office and got fifty dollars out. Got my ticket, I had five dollars left. Headed on a three day, two-night journey on the bus; I'm gonna leave it in the hand of the Lord. I'm leaving this place simply because I need to make a way for my family. It's raining, my dad couldn't work, man we stopped. I get to wondering right now, you know.

MOVING TO THE PROMISED LAND

I came to California in 1957, I left Mississippi Thursday morning an' I arrived in Los Angeles Saturday evening. I got to the bus station, I wrote my cousin a letter and told him I'm on my way, meet me there, I'm going to get there a certain time. I got there they wasn't there. I waited a couple of hours. Like downtown Mississippi somebody was down there every day, all day long. All you got to do is show up and you'll see somebody you know. And I thought it was that way out here cause so many people had left Mississippi and came out here. I waited but not so, people don't go downtown in Los Angeles, too many other cities. I waited a couple of hours and they didn't show up so I took a taxicab. I asked the taxi if he would take me to this address. It was on Leighton Street, I never will forget it. He said yes, I said what you charge me. He said three dollars. Ok let's go I got two dollars left and that was to last me 'til I find a job. We rode half the night 'til about twelve o'clock. He turned his machine off. He said, "Well do your folk have money?" I said, "Yes he works for Lockheed Aircraft." He said, "Oh I know where that is, I live out there by Lockheed Aircraft". He said, "I'll tell you what I'll do, I'll take you there". He took me; we were looking and couldn't find it. I had never read a map in my life. I looked and I finally saw it. I said, "here it is right here". He said, "oh yeah I don't know why I couldn't see it". We went on to the house; my cousin had two boys. I knew that they was home that year. I told them I was coming. When I got to the place it was about twelve at night, I saw two little boys running, the door was open. I saw them playing. I jumped out the taxicab. I ran into the house. Almost scared these folks to death, then I told right quick who I was, where I was from and who I was looking for. That lady remembered the letter, my name was on the letter. She remembered my cousin she said, "Oh yes I know that lady, they moved but I know where she move". Thank God she knew where she moved. She said, "I got some mail here for them". She let me get it. She got the mail and gave it to me. There was the letter that I wrote my cousin to come downtown. They had never picked up the mail.

Then we went on to the house where my cousin was. We got to the house about two o'clock in the morning. I knocked on the door. She answered the door and asked who it was. I told her who I was. She said, "wait a minute and I'll open the door". She jumped up and opened the door. She grabbed me. I said, "Do you got any money?" She said, "No my husband is working but he'll be here in the morning, what you need? I said, "I need to get my luggage". I had one little ole suitcase; all of the leather had worn off the suitcase tied up with hay bale wire. I don't know what the cabdriver thought about me. One of the poorest persons you ever saw in your life. But look at God! But God! So I went back and told the taxi, I said, "My cousin is working, his wife don't have no money but we will come pick it up tomorrow".

Cousin: Reverend Norman Clark

He gave me his address and my cousin took off work the next day. It took me to this man's house and got my suitcase. My cousin took me all over Hollywood, Beverly Hills all over. He showed me the most beautiful places I had never saw in my life. It was just like paradise, it was just like heaven to me. I heard about it, I saw it on TV occasionally, still didn't see the real realness of it 'til I was it with my eyes. I fell in love with the place. That's going on 44 years and a half. And I went on back to his house; I stayed with my cousin who was a preacher.

Now I got to have a job. I went round to his brother's house. His brother's wife gave me a job to cut her lawn. And that money she paid me four or five dollars but it lasted me to go out and look for a job. I went out that Monday, the man gave me a job that Monday. And that money she gave me lasted me until I got enough money to make it from that point on. I was so excited to have a job; the man saw me work he just fell in love with my work. And I been working ever since. Worked forty-four and a half years and was not out of work not one day in my life. I'm telling you something!

So what happened then I was staying with my cousin, I got a job now making money. He took me down to Watts at Martin's store, co-signed for me some clothes, some shoes, bought me some nice stuff, cause that suit I had I wore two or three times and it was brown and turned red on me. Then I bought my mother her first nice outfit. I bought her the whole suit, the coat, shoes, purse everything and sent it back to her. She was so excited that I did that for her.

That first Sunday morning after I arrived here, I went to church with him and the following Sunday and I joined up with Good Faith Baptist Church. An' this pastor, he treated me like I was one of the ministers of the church; he treated me with so much love. An' I really appreciate this man of God, we call . . . , I'm not gon' call his real name but we call him Rev, but he was really a great Rev.

I was a gospel singer, a quartet singer. I left the Southland gospel singers that I was singing with until we made professional. Then I came out here that's when the group busted up. After I came out here I started singing with the Ohio Wonders; then I met one of the baddest group that I ever met in my life. They would shout the house called the Songs of Grace. We would walk into any church and turn it out they was that bad. Had one of the short guys who would shake his leg, and say, "you know, you know I wouldn't take nothing from my journey now". But there was something about that group that you had to learn about, we had to learn the hard way. In that something was, we saw two men who had towels and they'd get to sweating and they wipe each other's face with the towels. We thought it was just a regular thing. They were getting ready to go on tour, I think it was Arizona somewhere out that way. They were making big time bucks. They were big timers. I wouldn't have to work if I had stayed with them. My cousin and I were (Walter James Brown) was my cousin, he was the lead singer, I could sing everything but bass. And I was the fifth singer they love that high voice. I could go up in the clouds. (singing "You better watch were you going to judgment day!) What happened was, I told them OK we going to be ready to go on that tour. And he said, "Well since y'all gonna be with us we have to tell you, this man and I is husband and wife". My cousin said, "Roosevelt, I don't think we ready for this understandin' I think we need to get outta here." We left that group and I start singing on my own.

I had went and joined Good Faith Baptist Church. An' this pastor, he was a gospel singer, and a gospel preacher an' a gospel man. This man taught me everything I know about church. When I came here, I came right offa the farm. I didn't even know what a pew was; I didn't know what an audience was. So he taught me how to talk and how to do things in the church. First of all he had me in training being a deacon, I stayed in training for a while; then I finally got it. Then he taught me how to conduct the devotion service; taught me how to pray and taught me how to talk to the audience. Then after I got on the way and learned how to do all that, then he taught me how to receive the offering from the people, not only that, he taught me how to give. Believe it or not this Baptist church was giving tithes and offering, that's the thing that the Baptist was not doing when I was in Mississippi; but he taught me everything.

He taught me how to sing with the choir when they went on their engagements, I was singing with the choir and they would request, every church that I went to, for me to get up and sing an' when I would get up and sing, they would get so excited they would be shouting all over the place. I mean the Lord moved in a mighty way.

Roosevelt at a Young Age

Then, I didn't even have the Holy Ghost, I just had the gift of singing. So, what happened; my cousin's wife didn't go to church that much with us but she went occasionally an' my cousin would go and preach so many churches after, . . after the service was out in the evening and I would sing for him and then I learned how to sing real good and I made that a standing. Then I went to his brother's house, who had some tapes an' . . . , and actually he had some records and I learned some songs by the Blind Boys, "I'm Gonna Leave you in the Hands of the Lord", "Someone Watching Over Me", an' the Lord blessed me with those songs an' they got to be a standard song for me, an' I began to sing those songs all over California.

SAVED, SANCTIFIED AND FILLED

So what happened, after I stayed at my cousin's so long, we would go, after our service was out every Sunday night, we would get out of church about . . h-m-m eight-thirty or nine o'clock and then we'd go 'round to that little sanctified church right around the corner from my cousin's house. Those people were shoutin', an' they was singing, an' preaching and praising God. So one night I was sitting there an' my cousin said to me, he said "Bro. Leggette, these people got something" and I say, "What they got?" He said, "Well, I don't know, but I think that they have the Holy Ghost" and he said, "One'ah these days I'm gonna receive the Holy Ghost."

Then I met the girl I wanted to be my wife walking down the street not too far from my house; she had a long pony tail light skin and tutoring everybody in the community only sixteen years old but she was very beautiful and I like that girl. I would try to talk to her and she wouldn't talk to me. Walk on the other side of the street. I didn't give up. Everybody would bring me girlfriends I didn't even like. But you have to like someone yourself. But not knowing that God was in the midst of this one day I met her on the same side of the street I was on.

And this particular day she didn't walk on the other side, she let me talk to her. Seemed like I had to tell her," Hey wait a minute girl, God sent me here for you". Seemed like that was what I was telling her. But anyway I don't know what I told her I was so excited. We finally start talking and she introduced me to her mother. She told me "My mother is sanctified, filled with the Holy Ghost".

I met her mother and she started preaching to me, I didn't know about bein' sanctified and holy. I had been to the church but when she started to talk to me, her hands would go up and I said, "Oh my God this woman's got it". She would preach to me; she had fell in love with me. Then basically I was going round to the house an' the whole family was so nice to me I fell in love with all of them; her other kids, her daughters, her sons. I was Baptist, but the oldest son, he treated me like I was a sanctified bishop. He treated me that way. And I'm gonna tell you what her mother told me one day, "You guys got to get your business together, you ought to get married. It's not good for young people to be just going around like this, it's not good".

So we decided we would get married and my girlfriend told me . . . , she told me that if I'm gonna get married to her, not only do you have to get the Holy Ghost but I'm gonna have to take you around to my church to meet my pastor". and he had to counsel with us. She took me to her church and let me meet Bishop Conedy. Sure enough he told me, "I don't let my girls go out and marry people that's not in the church". The same faith that they was in. And he counseled with me and he said to me, he say, "Well, you gonna get married anyway you might's well go and do it right and be not unequally yoked up together" . . Receive the Holy Ghost", He say "It's just that easy, all you gotta do is just receive the Holy Ghost and then you'll be ready to live a marriage life." Unh, I didn't get upset with him because I felt like he was telling me the right thing.

So I went on and I start tarrying for the Holy Ghost. I was all 'round in the bathroom tarrying trying to receive it, trying to receive; so it didn't come. I was all around the house trying to get the Holy Ghost, in the bathroom and the kitchen all over the house singing, I was singing all the time anyway.

One lady next door said her radio broke down and she tuned me in. She loved to hear me sing. I sang all the time but it didn't come. So but I knew I was going to get the Holy Ghost.

So I would go to church and on Sunday night after we'd get out of our church I would wear the worsest thing I had because I didn't want to be rolling and tumbling in my clean pretty stuff, 'cause I had finally had my cousin to sign a note for me to get some clothes and I had some pretty good clothes and I didn't want to get them all wrinkled and dirty and what have you.

So Reverend Clark told me he said, "Brother Leggette It's something those people have cause there ain't no way in the world they could go along that long shoutin', hollerin' and screamin' hours like that. They got something." He said, "Brother Leggette they got the Holy Ghost. One of these days I'm gonna get it." He a Baptist preacher, he's preachin' and I'm signing for him. We travelin' all over the city. So finally forty-four and a half years later, ain't that long ago, he received the Holy Ghost. But to make my long story short, I have a little sister by the name of sister Olivia Ash, she's a big time missionary. And the churches that she's over right now, she has about forty-six churches under her.

And then I was braggin' to my cousins, I was makin' fun of the sanctified folks. I said "Ya'll hear me hollerin', comin' down the street, I got that thing." I was just talking you know; and sure enough Elder

Stewart came by, I was sitting on the front seat. He came up the aisle laying hands on people praying for them. They was fallin' out, foaming at the mouth. "My God", I said "my gracious, it's gonna

Apostle J.E. Steward and Wife   Carrie Steward

be my turn after a while, I wonder if something gonna happen to me like that?" Then all in my mind I say, "I'm gonna be nice about it, I'm not gonna fall out like that, I'm just gonna receive mine." That's what I had in mind. But don't you know as I was sitting on the mo'ning bench, that's the front seat; Elder Steward was walking down the aisle laying hands on the people saying, "Bless'em Lord, Bless'em Lord" that's all he was saying. "Bless'em Lord, Bless'em Lord". Then I-I saw him comin' close to me an' I was nervous, I didn't . . . I didn't know what the Holy Ghost was and I didn't know what it was gonna do, but I saw the people leaping and shouting and slobbering at the mouth an' . . . an' speaking in tongues and I say; "Well, I wonder what gon' happen to me when, when this . . . , when he lay hands on me," and I was just trying to figger it out.

I had already told my cousin when I left home, when I left the house, "I,m goin' 'round to that sanctified church and if you hear me hollering and screaming and going on, I have that thing." And,. sho' Nuff, he laid hands on me and something struck me, hit me in the top of my head, ran all the way down to the bottom of my feet and it knocked me completely out. I was laying there completely out and the pastor said I was out for two hours under the conviction of the Holy Ghost.

And after I received the Holy Ghost, there was a lady by the name of Thelma Johnson, an' when I—I would get to church before she would, an' when I see her coming in the door I would start rolling and tumbling and speaking in tongues. So I eased up to her one night; I say, "Mother, I wanna know one thing," I say, "Am I gonna be able to just sit and talk with you one of these days without all this carrying on?" She said, "Son," she say," you will be able to control it," she say, "this is the anointing of the Holy Ghost." From that point on I knew I received the Holy Ghost. Then I finally got where I could control it. But what I was about to say; when that thing hit me I was on my way home and I was leaping and I was like the man at the beautiful gate begging for alms. Like Peter and John raised him up. I went down the street leaping and shouting and praising God. One o'clock in the morning, people didn't know what in the world was happening. But that Holy Ghost had me.

I got up to work the next morning. I went to work like that speaking in tongues the next morning. Then I was telling my supervisor about what happened to me. But he was an atheist, he didn't believe in God. He said, "Man you crazy, I like you, you a good man, you a good worker but you are so pitiful you don't know what's going on. You talking 'bout you got some kind of holy ghost or something. You talking about there is a god or something." I said,

"There is a God". I tried to convince him cause it happened to me, I said, "It's working all through me now". My supervisor was working for this man who was Armenian and Armenians believe in going to church. And this Armenian man that owned the company had a son-in-law that was working there. And this son-in-law believed me so strongly and he was one of those mean Italians and he didn't like the supervisor so well. So he told me he said "If you say again that there is not a God and you don't believe what Roosevelt is saying I'll knock your brains out". I had to step between them and say, "Wait a minute, let's don't fight about this thing. It's real whether you guys believe it or not or want to fight about it or not, it's real. Let's just leave it like that, let's not make a big thing of it". From that point on the Lord blessed me.

MARRIAGE: A NEW STEP

S o, back to the story of my wife. I had met this young lady. I asked her let's get married, I got the Holy Ghost now, I'm ready. You young men that want to live a Christian life and want to be married, receive the Holy Ghost and make sure your mate receives the Holy Ghost, make sure she can cook. My pastor took me to my wife's god mothers house and we got married about 1 o'clock AM after church service was out.

God blessed us to move into a little duplex house. We had a rough time trying to get furniture. We had to get second hand furniture, mismatched furniture, dresser one color, the bed one color, the end table one color, the table one color. But we moved in and we didn't have enough money to buy groceries. I told my wife, "You go and stay with your mother and I will go and stay with my cousin until I get some money". She said, "If you stay in a one room shack I want to stay there with you." That's what she told me. So we had one brother of the church, Elder Lyles, who gave us ten dollars for a marriage gift. We took that ten dollars and bought enough groceries to last us 'til the end of the week 'til I got paid cause I was already working so I had a check coming.

And then what happened we sent and got my mother and brought her all the way from Meridian, Mississippi. She got a live in job and started staying. After a while, she and I got together and we sent and got all of my younger brothers and sisters first. Got another duplex house 'cause that little ole house I was livin' in was too small. And with a hall down the middle we put my mother and my sisters and brothers on one side; my wife and I lived on the other side of the house.

I'm doing good now, trying to do good. Done a whole lot for my family. Went to work and came back and they done jumped on my wife. That's the first time I got mad at my real family. I felt like kicking them all out but I couldn't do that. My cousin gave me a house then, where Martin Luther King hospital is now. I packed up and moved my mother and them into that house and then I rented a house. I stayed in that house for a couple of years.

HOW I BOUGHT MY HOUSES

Then I went to Compton saw a house that I liked, told the man what I wanted to do. I liked the house and let's go inside and take a look at it. I looked at it, he had a little suit case and I said how much do you want for it. He said I want a thousand down, I want nine five for it and I want a thousand down. That leaves eight five. Ok a two bedroom house nice, beautiful. Don't you know I didn't have a thousand dollars? He said, "Well how do expect to buy this house if you ain't got no money down". I said, "If I tell you how to sell this house to me would you sell it to me?" He said "Sure". He said, "Well what do you want to do Mr. Leggett?" I said, "What I want you to do is, how much you want?" He said, "I want nine thousand five hundred". I said, "Raise it up a thousand" He said, "Ok ten five" I said, "Ok, subtract a thousand". He said" OK". I said, "I just gave you a thousand". He said, "Man you crazy, that ain't gone to work" I said let's try it and see.

We took it to the mortgage company and it went through like hot cakes. He sold me another one like that. Then he sold some more people houses like that all over the place, like I said before; I moved right up the street, I bought another one. I got four houses now. Then I got rid of one of the other houses that he let me have then I got rid of the one on Martin Luther King. Then I had a lady give me a three-bedroom house with nothing down that was Ruth Atlas' sister. All I had to do was take it over and pay off a little bill she had on a counter top she had built in the kitchen. A three bedroom house, that was like thirty something years ago. I yet have that house now. My oldest daughter's been living in it for over twenty years. She yet living there now my oldest daughter Gretchen, a beautiful three bedroom house. Then I decided . . . , well, we were living in that house and the school district got so bad in Compton. They were raping teachers with brick bats at twelve o'clock and they we cutting kids' fighting gang members, killing kids. So we moved our address on the school records and moved them over to Downey where my sister-in law was living we used her address and they caught us there so we ran for it I moved to Riverside. So I saw this five-bedroom house way out here in Riverside, sixty-five miles away.

Before we go there, let me tell you about how I got involved in the this sanctified church.

WORKING OUT MY SOUL'S SALVATION

Now after I received the Holy Ghost at that little sanctified church around the corner from my cousin's house, I joined up with Pastor J.E. Steward there. Pastor Steward took me and placed me in his church in position. First of all he made me a deacon and then he made me, uh—one of the choir members and as time passed he said to me, "Brother Leggette, I want you to be my head deacon." I said, :Well I . . . uh don't see how I can do that 'cause there are a lot of deacons much older than I am and uh-I feel like that I would be out of my place trying to do their position. He said, "Well, I want to let you know this, the pastor appoints deacons and God saved the deacon and then when the pastor appoints'em, then I'll teach you everything you need to know about being the deacon." Then I say, "Why you want me to be your head deacon?" Then he say, "You meet all the qualifications. You pay your tithes, you pay your offering and you at church all the time and you do what I tell you to do." So I accepted the appointment for deacon, I accept that an' the Lord blessed me in a marvelous way. So I stayed there for about almost ten years under the leadership of Pastor Steward and the Lord healed me from certain ailments. I had eye problems since I was real young, wore real thick glasses, and he healed my eyes through Pastor Steward an' my eyes stayed healed for 'bout thirty some years, didn't have to wear no glasses. I'm blind now but it's not because of that. This is something else, but the Lord blessed me to stay there with Ol' Saint Joe and work. I was a Sunday School Superintendent and I worked with YPWW. Everything I found my hand to do I did it and the Lord blessed me; All-Righty!

So Elder Steward left the church and the church ended. When he left the church, I . . left too, 'cause I didn't have a leader to follow; so I didn't stay with Elder Pearce. Willie Pearce was our Junior Pastor, uh—our assistant pastor too. You might's well say that, but still I am a, uh—professionally I'm a member of Elder Pearce's church; that's New Jerusalem number two, so I didn't change my membership when I left there and went to . . . we crossing over now.

Supt. Willie Pearce and Wife,   Sis Carrie Pearce

I went to New Jerusalem Church of God in Christ and I joined up with them the first Sunday I got there, that first Sunday night. And Elder Jones asked me, he say, "Brother Leggette, what can you do? What did you do at your other church?" I explained to him that I was the head deacon and I worked with the brothers in the men's department and then I knew about working with the pastor's aid. So what he did was, he placed me as a pastor's aide president; his wife worked with me and I was one of the greatest men's day pastor's aide president that you ever want to see. The reason I was so successful was, because his wife always came up with programs and helped me . . and helped me implement the program. And she worked with me and I was number one.

So then he turned around and made me a deacon. I worked with . . , after I learned the way they did the deacon, I worked with the deacons, all the deacons. Then he looked at me and he said, "Brother Leggette, I think I want you to be my head deacon," he said. I said, "Well I understand it," and I said, "When I left, uh, under Saint Joseph I was the head deacon and I know how it's supposed to be done" and he said, "Well, okay, I want you to try it."

I, uh, accepted the calling and I accepted the offer and then I start working with it. So we had about thirty brothers; Uh, I said to him, I said, "Pastor Jones," I said, "You the pastor an' I'm not trying to change things but, . . ." I say "But, the Bible said bring ye your tithes and offering into the storehouse so there will be meat in my house, an' I will open a window and pour out a blessing, there won't be enough room to receive it. But you said if you don't give tithes, give a good offering." An' I said, "But Pastor Jones, that's not biblical", I said, "The Bible didn't say it like that. I'm not trying to be contrary to your leadership." He said, "I . . . , it didn't say . . . what does it say? I said, "Just what I just said." I said, "I tell you what I want you to do. You don't have no business working a job and trying to pastor this big church," an' I say, "You're getting of age now; you need to retire." He say, "Brother Leggette, I cain't retire, I cain't depend on these people, they'll starve you to death." I say, "Give me a chance to show you what I can do," an' he said, "Okay, okay, go for it." So I say, "Let me have my way with the brothers and we'll do it the Bible way an' I'll have all the brothers to come and work with me; an' then we'll start giving tithes and then the Lord will bless this work, 'cause that's what He said He would do." He say," Oh well, go for it."

I called a meeting; I called all the brothers, all the deacons and all the preachers together, then we met in the upper room. It was about twenty-five or thirty of us and then I let'em know what I had in mind, what I was gonna try, an' I wanted them to work with me. They say, "Well," then I say, "Can you guys work with me on this?" They said, "What you want to do?" "We gonna try giving tithes and offering, 'an we gonna see what's gonna happen. The Bible say it will bless us." They said okay an' I-I got about . . . 'I had them to raise their hands and I got about three-fourths of 'em to raise their hands that say that they were gonna work with me. So after that; we say okay, we gonna try it on the first Sunday; every first Sunday was pastoral Sunday an' they said okay.

On the first Sunday we tried it and the offering came up about three times the amount that it was normally be, and that let us know that the God was really working. And I went to the pastor and I talked to him and I said, "Did you check the offering out today?" and he said, "Yeah!" I said, "How much more we got now than we normally get?" He said, "You got about three times as much." I said, "This is tithes;" I said, "Now you gonna have more than that when you get the women's involved." He said, "Brother Leggette, it's really working, it's really working." I said, "The Bible said it's gonna work! You said it's gonna work; you been preaching that." An', uh, I said okay.

I called another meeting and then when I got up told the brothers that whenever you get up to take the offering, you tell about how the Lord has blessed you for giving your tithes. They started that, then the sisters, then I said we want all the church to start giving tithes. Right now we had about three-fourths of the brothers giving an' I say we want you sisters to stand with us brothers 'cause we brothers want to lead out like a man and let the Lord bless us. The sisters start giving so now we're getting four or five times as much as we were getting. So, now Elder Jones was so excited; I got with the assistant pastor and I said we got to retire this pastor. We raised so much money every first Sunday until he said, "Brother Leggette, I'm getting more money now than I was getting even with what I was getting before and also my salary." He said, "I think I will retire."

Pastor J.D. Jones and wife, Sister Dollie Mae Jones

He retired and then I stayed with New Jerusalem for almost twenty-one years. Yet, I gave in the offering, I gave good every time I got up; I'm not patting myself on the back, an' I am. I would talk about how the Lord blessed and the people caught on.

One lady caught on so much so; she met me in the parking lot, she said, "you said if you give your tithes and offering the Lord would bless you. And they praying . . . they were praying that He would bless you thirty, sixty and a hundred fold." And I said, "Yeah, that's right!" an' she said, "Now I wanna give my tithes, if I give my tithes, uh . . . , how long you think it'll take for me to get my blessing? I wanna pay my rent and I need a thousand dollars so if I give a hundred dollars then the Lord bless me a hundred times see how much I would have?" Then I said well, "You got the wrong impression. A lotta times the Lord may not bless you in money, He may bless you in spiritual blessings, He might bless you with health, He might bless your kids." I say, "Don't look at it like that! You look at it like, . . . you look at it like, I'm gonna give and whatever the Lord gives me back, I know it's gonna be good. I'm gonna be thankful."

So I stayed there and worked with them and every anniversary, I was the head of the anniversary and we had a rally going on and the men and the sisters, we all got together, we raised so much money til' New Jerusalem got to be one of the greatest churches in Compton. We called it the dignified sanctified church. They all had businesses, had new cars, homes, an' I mean God was blessin' em every way, we never saw it like that. So I stayed there for about uh . . , twenty-one years as I said after Pastor J.D. Jones, Pastor J.T. Jones took over the Church.

Pastor J.T. Jones and Evangelist Mary D. Jones

MOVING TO A BETTER PLACE

Then I decided I would move to Riverside; moved out here and bought a nice five bedroom house. I went to visit with my brother-in-law, Elder Ash, an' went 'round to his friend's an' his friend was telling us about a house was down the street there for sale and I said I'm lookin' for a house, I wanna move out here." So what he said was, "Well, go down and take a look at it." I went and took a look at it, I liked it, I saw the man and I told him what I would do. An' I say, "I want that house!" He say . . , then I say, "How much you want down on it?" Then he say "I want three thousand dollars," an' he said, "I'm leaving out of town; I'm going to Mississippi, my wife wanna go and stay with her mother then, uh . . that's where we goin'. I tell you what I'll do; I'll let you have this house and when I get back you can give me my three thousand dollars." I say, "Okay." That give me time to . . , about three months to work to get the money together. When he came back, I didn't have the three thousand dollars but he came up, an' I said, "Mister you had about five thousand dollars worth of furniture around the pool, an' it's all gone," an' I say, "You got some cracked windows upstairs." I say, "You didn't keep your end of the bargain." I said, "Now, uh . . . we had, that was an agreement that you was gonna leave me the pool furniture, I could sue you for

39

breechin' the agreement." He said, "Well look, my wife was a good Samaritan and she gave the furniture to all of the neighborhoods," and I said, "that was not in the plan." He said, "Okay, you just go ahead keep it and forget about it, forget about you owe me anything and he left town." Then he came back a little while later and he said, "Do you have a picture of the house?" I said yes and he gave me about ten dollars for the picture. He said, "I want to take it back to Mississippi to let my people see it." He left and I haven't saw him since. So I came on, I moved on out here and then I . . . I was in the house for about uh, oh . . . almost a year and I felt like, that I was not, I wudn't, I wudn't the owner of the house 'cause the way I didn't put nothing down. Then I got kinda like . . . , I got kinda like shaky and I decided, I would go and check it out. I had a title search on it and it was nothing on it and then I found out that it was my house; the Lord had blessed me with that house.

From that point on . . . , at that time I had a plot of land in California City and I got rid of that. Then I went and bought myself four vacation homes. The first one I bought was in Palm Springs, the next one was in San Diego near Lawrence Welk's, the next one was on top of a hill in Big Bear, and the next one was by Ontario airport. Right now I don't want you all to feel sorry for me. Because of my wife, the way she handled the money, I let her handle the money. She was a manager, she managed the money. I went out and dug it up and gave it to her and she put it in the right place. Right now we are doing well because of my wife. Don't feel sorry for me. I was crying because of the way I was brought up. Right now, I am not working. I am on social security and disability. I'm drawing enough each month to sustain me. God is supplying our needs. Don't feel sorry for me I have no hard luck story. I want to let you all know that if you expect to get anywhere in life, my secret was for livin' . . . was : I'd give God his part first then I would go out and get what I wanted. That means pay your tithes and offerings and be a blessing to God's people.

I need to tell you some more about what happened in Mississippi before we finish the remainder of the church.

MOTHER, FATHER AND FAMILY IN CALIFORNIA

After my mom and sisters and brothers stayed out here a while we sent back and got my father. He came out here, still don't have a hard luck story. Then my oldest brother in Florida passed about a couple of years after I was out here. We flew him here and buried him. Then my next brother died, then my father died, then my mother died. Boy they leavin' huh? Then one of my little sisters passed away, Georgia, she was child number seven. Then my oldest sister died, she was child number four under me. When I lost my mother I thought sure I couldn't make it but I got my oldest sister, my little mama, my oldest sister. Now I hardly got a little something to hold on to. Ol' Deff' came by and took her. I thought . . . , I gave up the ghost, I gave up to leave here. I told Sister LaVette "This is it. I can't make it now. I took all I can take. I can't take no more. I can't make it." She screamed at me. She said "Brother Leggette, you can make it, you have a beautiful family, you got a wife, sisters and brothers to live for." She hit me, look like she shook me, something broke loose on the inside of me. Gave me a brand new hope on life and I've been going strong ever since. Every time I look at sister LaVette she seem like one of the greatest persons in the whole world.

I mean she is a beautiful lady but I can't even see that. She's just somebody that is really super special. I want you to know, people help people. We have to be there for one another.

I am going to add some more to this testimony as time go on but don't take it lightly. The time that you have is very important. At the end of my journey I want somebody to know what happened to me during my coming up in life.

Down through the years I had it hard, I had it so hard. Coming on up through the years I made it on over. God said, "Don't cry no more". I had to cry in the midnight hour but I made it, I made it on over. May God bless you. Yours truly. Break

I'm so glad that the Lord saved me. If it had not been for Jesus, I wonder right now where would I be. What we're going to do now is, we are going to continue our story 'A testimony for the past tense of my life'. My father unfortunately, lost his health at a very early age. I want you to know one thing, my dad when he was a young man not even fifty years old, he lost his health. He was in a wheel chair the last part of his life. My father was paralyzed from his waist down, couldn't walk. My father and I didn't get along that well neither did he get along good with any of his children. He was the kind of person would cuss every word he say. Look like for some reason he just didn't like me and I was the best worker in his house. I'd do everything he asked me. He called me my mother's black Jesus. He and I didn't get along good at all. None of the children could get along with him. When he come in the front door we all would go out the back. That was the kind of life we lived. My dad was so mean to us and my mother. That was the reason my mother called me, wrote a letter to me and told me she just couldn't take no more of him. She wanted to come to California where I was. That's why I sent for her.

But before I left Mississippi, with this TV screen that I have, that the Lord blessed me with, (I can see things in the future what's gonna happen.) I saw my dad getting sick. I saw the sickness coming up on him before it happened. I looked at him that morning, I told him; I said, "Dad I'm leaving town. I'm going to make the conditions better for you all. But I'm going to leave this with you, if you don't change your way of living, when I see you again I'm not gonna know you." He looked at me, I didn't know whether he was gonna knock my head off or whatever, but I had to tell him. It was hard but I just had to tell him. So after sending to get my mother, my sisters and my brothers, I started to leave him down there. Let him make it the best way he could. I felt he never done nothing for me. But the little that he did for me, if he hadn't did that little in my childhood, I know it would have been even worse or rougher for me. So I sent for him. When I met him at the bus station, [oh glory to God!] I didn't know my dad, he was in such a bad condition, trying to walk, dragging one leg, real poor. I didn't know him. But you know, I tell you this, I had that love in my heart for people. I didn't have that much love in my heart for him. I want to tell you the truth on this story, I didn't care nothing about my dad. But you know what? When my dad died, I funeralized him, I guess I took it easier than anybody simply because I did everything I could for him and them.

Young people let me tell you something, treat your dad right, treat your mother right. (I want you to hear this song in the background, don't you hear it?) One day I was in the bedroom after I buried my father and I was taking it real good, his death. But something hit me over my head like a hammer. I didn't know whether I cared anything about my dad at all. I don't know what that was. That grief hit me so hard until I fell in the closet. My wife was looking at me. I fell in the closet, I just cried it out, I just laid there, she didn't bother me. Then when I got up it looked like to me that was the best thing that ever happened to me, let all that pressure out.

Young people regardless of how your dad and momma treat you, listen at this song, you treat them nice. I credit that to my living for so long because the way I took care of my dad. I took him in my brand new Cadillac, I rode him all over the city. A lot of times I wasn't able to take him to his appointments at the hospital, my wife would take him.

One of my houses had caught on fire, burned partially down. I put that house back together. My mother began staying in that house. When I completed it (my Dad was in the hospital), I went and told my dad. I said, "Dad the house is completed now an' when you get out of this hospital (I'm not gonna to cry today y'all, I got tears running down my face now but that's not real tears that's just something happening, it's just doing it). I said "Dad the house is ready now". I'm just talking to him just normally, like I normally talk to him. He said, "Roosevelt, I'm gon' tell you this, I'm gon' pay you the rent this month," he said "but I'm not gon' pay no more. One thing my dad said to me when I was visiting him in the hospital (I've always cared a lot about my family). You make them boys take care of the rent. You make Henry and Gene take care of it. They taking all of my county money to pay the rent but this is it". Listening to my dad talk, I thought he was telling me that 'hey, I'm gone to keep my money in my pocket. I'm gone to let them big boys pay it now. I'm not gone to pay no more. I'm not gone to carry them any longer'. That's the way I looked at it. I said, "Dad, don't worry about it. Oh the house looks so good, I wish you could see it", I said," you're going to see it though". But he didn't act interested in that at all. He acted as though I wasn't even talking to him. He was acting like 'hey you're just joking that's not important now'.

Then I went on home. That next morning before day my brother called and said my dad was dead. Oh, I almost cried that time but I'm holding it. I'm strong now y'all. I got me some power. Huh? I went on and buried my dad. I had one preacher, Elder Steward told me, he said, "Brother Leggette, your father's gone now but your mother is yet here. You guys can show us how much of a man you all are. It's five of you boys now, you can show us how much of a man you are by taking care of your mother and your sisters. When my mother moved into the house, I took her to the furniture store and I furnished the house off. I went back and helped her dig up the back yard; it was a big back yard, real rich. She planted her garden. She had collard greens, mustard greens, tomatoes, okra; you name it, it was a top of the line garden. I helped as much as I could. I made her a home there for as long as she lived. My mother lived there for almost ten years.

I want all you young folk to listen to me now. You know that every time you do a little something for your mother, your father, your sister, your brother; even your own kids, you charge them just like they are somebody out in the streets. I'm a tell you something, my daddy didn't teach us that much but one thing he taught us: don't charge your mother, father, sisters and brothers, your family for nothing. I have a commercial video business now. My wife and kids get upset with me sometimes because every time I do a wedding, a birthday thing or a church thing for my family I won't charge them at all. I just do it for free. But they tell me that's not the way to do business. But let me tell you something, God is blessing me. Every time I do that I take my wife and tell her, "Honey watch this one. I'm planting this seed, watch this seed. Sure enough it came to pass in front of our eyes. Maybe ten times or a hundred times more than what I gave to them it comes back to me and I reap the benefits of it.

SAD MEMORIES OF THE SOUTH

I want you to know one thing, when I was living in the country, (I want to keep these two stories close together.) One of the most saddest things that happened to us, one night my mother woke us up in the middle of the night. She told us to run outside quick, the house was no fire. We all ran around her and I've always been a person that was concerned about the family. Basically, I was the oldest one around her at that particular time because my oldest brother was not that concerned. I looked up at mother and I said, "Mother what are we gone to do now? Everything we have is gone". My mother looked down at us and she looked up towards heaven and she stretched out her hands and she said "Father I stretch my hands to thee. No other help I know. If you would withdraw yourself from me right now I wonder where would I go". The people around in the community gathered around looking at the fire burning up everything we had.

The white man gave us another house to stay in. We had friends, this is what you call neighbors. Some would come and bring us a sheet. Some would come and bring a pillow. Some would come and bring a quilt. Some would come and bring a bed frame. My dad would go and get some lumber and make what you call slats put across the bed, put the bed frame on it, put the mattress on it, some would give us mattresses. Some would give us dishes and some would give us clothes and at the end we had more than what we had in the beginning. Then we started a new life all over again but that mark went with us for a long time. Everybody in the school house, they knew that we got burnt out. They would say, "Rosy'n'em house caught on fire and burned up everything that they had." They didn't laugh at us. It was a struggle until we got everything we needed 'cause money was a tight thing then. Nobody couldn't give us no money. They would be coming from everywhere; kill a hog, give us what you call a mess of meat, some would be bringing us peas, greens, everything that we didn't really have they would come and give to us.

MEMORIES OF THE WAR

Another thing I'd like to let you know in this, uh . . . story, we black people back in the South could identify with each other because we all had the same lifestyle. We all didn't have nothing and we was all operating under the same mean taskmaster, which was the white man. One time we had a war and they were rationing sugar, but the man that we were working with, the man we live with on his farm, he would come to our house and bring us sugar, those brown eggs that they would give us and give us that flour and give us meal, an' . . . but what happen was, he was getting it free, but we would have to pay him for it. We would just put it on the charge account in his store, so we had plenty of food now, 'cause the war was going on. Things was really tight.

We saw the CC boys come marching down through the fields, we saw that. But we were blessed and I . . . I didn't ever want to go to the army, I wanted to go to California or Springfield, Massachusetts one or the other and get my family into a better environment, get 'em outta Mississippi, just anything. So—this particular year, they called me to be examined for the army. We was, we was living in Meridian, (about 18 miles north of Meridian, out in the country).

I caught the bus and went on to Jackson, Mississippi, they took care of that. I was examined and I passed; I didn't want to go to the war. I had cousins that went to the army and they came back, some of 'em crazy, uh . . . alcoholics an' acting all crazy and I just didn't wanna go. There was a lady right in that little . . . there was a little place called Daleville, three or four stores and this lady, we had a Post Office and she asked me do you want to go to the army. I said no I don't wanna go but they say, uh . . . I passed. She filled out a questionnaire for me. She wrote on that questionnaire that I was the second oldest of twelve kids and that my mother needed my presence to help take care of the family and that lady mailed that letter in and they reclassified me to 4-F. When I got reclassified to 4-F, that's when I caught the bus coming to California. 'Cause I knew right then I was outta danger. So all the white people around there in that particular town said to me, they said, "Little Jodie, if you get out there and can't make, all you got to do is write me a letter and I'll send you a ticket back here. That was nice, But I said . . . but I was saying in my mind, I'm not ever coming back here to stay anymore.

I came to California and after I stayed about ten years, then I went back and I saw the home-boy, the young man that I grew up with. His father and mother was old and he was taking over the farm. He promised to build me a brand new house if I would just come back and help him take care of his cattle, his farm and everything, and he would've done it 'cause we grew up together, we was really good friends. I told him I couldn't go, I couldn't come back, because I had too much property in California; I was really tied down. He even had a meat market right in front of the place where we used to live, but what happened was I knew I had too much to lose out here and my memory . . . the memories were too great; I wouldn't never be able to deal with it anymore. It got too cold there, too rainy, too much everything. So California was, like sunny California, money grow on trees, living out here got nice homes, making good money, got a beautiful family; wasn't no way I could give that up 'cause I had too much bad memory.

My Cousin's Death

One really bad memory I had was about a cousin. We had this cousin that lived not too far from us, (back in the South the people; the white people would take your land away from you by paying the taxes on your land) So what happened, for two or three years in a row they paid the taxes on my cousin's land, I don't believe he even knew they were paying it. But they came in possession of his land because they paid the taxes and they asked my cousin to move. My cousin said, "White folks, this is my land." They said, "No it's not your land, this land belong to us." My cousin said, "No white folks, this land belongs to me, I was born on this land, my fore-parents gave it to me. In fact they gave all of us a share, my brothers and sisters have a share in this land." He said, "Please let me stay here on my land." They said. "No, we want you to be out of here—by tomorrow." So he got nervous; back in the country when people got nervous they would smoke a lot, more than normal, dip snuff or chew tobacco more than was normal, or drink alcohol. My cousin's house had a fireplace built on to it, like the fireplaces we have out here in California. But he had a shelf over the fireplace, the shelf was about six feet high, about five and a-half or six feet high, that's the way they built them back there in the country. He kept his snuff box on the shelf. So he walked over to the shelf, he got nervous and he reached up (Whoo! I'm not gonna cry on this one) an' he reached up to get his snuff box; those white folks shot him down in cold blood and took the land. We thought there was something we could do about it but they had an excuse that my cousin was reaching for a gun and this was something that was self-defense, and there wasn't anything we could do about it.

WORKING THE COTTON FIELD; CUTTING PUCKWOOD

N ow I was a good worker, when I went out in anybody's cotton field, I was the champion. They would put up a "Bo Dollar". The one that picked the most cotton would get that "Bo Dollar." The "Bo Dollar" and the Silver Dollar was two different things. Every day!! Five days a week, six days a week, whatever, I took the "Bo Dollar," I picked five hundred pounds of cotton and over. And the people couldn't understand why I would be picking right along there with them with my two rows and when I get out to the end and I would weigh up fifteen to twenty pounds more than them. When they'd get so far behind what I would do was . . , they was my good friends, I would get on their row and go back . . . , pick back, pick back, and catch 'em up so they could stay up with me and that counted when I got to the end of the row. Sometimes I would . . . (Listening to music, "How long has it been since you talked to the Lord?") Sometimes when I get at the end of the row it would be almost . . ., quitting time ; we worked from sunup to sundown. When the sun go down, getting ready to go, they would hammer on a plow, let you know that it's quitting time.

Sometime I'd get to the end of the row and I'd have four hundred and ninety pounds; I need ten more pounds to make five hundred.

What I would do is, I would rush back out in the field; everybody sitting there, they counting, they weighing up the cotton, you got about twenty people you weighing their cotton. An' I'd let 'em weigh mine up first and I'd rush back out in the field and by time they'd get through weighing up everybody's cotton an' paying everybody off, then I'd come back in and weigh mine; they would let me do it, because I was trying to . . . set a record.

Nobody could beat me anyway, I had everybody beat anyhow, then I'd go back out and I'd get like . . . fifteen to twenty pounds; that'd put me over . . . the five hundred mark; but I'd already got my Silver Dollar; my "Bo Dollar." Then I would go home and I did that year after year after year, but I want to let people know what I felt was my secret to success is, that I would thank God every time I'd weigh up a sack, all day long.

And . . . but when it come . . ., when I finished the cotton season, then I'd go out in the woods and work with the people that was cutting logs, we cut paper wood. The paper wood was about five foot, three inches, I won't forget that, 'cause they was big around.

What they . . . those logs weighed about two hundred fifty to three hundred pounds, took two or three people to pick that log up and put it on their shoulders and you walk with it to the truck. So the people that came out here from Mississippi they got old, they suffer with back trouble, everything, they health just went away. But thank God I didn't put all my life in that kinda work so my . . . I didn't have that kinda big problem.

So, but one thing my dad taught me how to be a wrestler. I was a wrestling champion, every school I went to, nobody could put me down. We didn't wrestle like they wrestle now, they do some crazy stuff now, they twist your arm off, try to break your neck and all that kinda crazy stuff and make you surrender. Way we would do it, we would just throw you down and the one who hit the ground the first was the loser. Nobody could put me down 'cause I had got used to . . . , got my body built body up toting those big logs and when I went to school those kids weren't used to that kinda thing. When they jumped on me, that was just like jumping on one those Brahma bulls. I would . . . , I would take 'em in the air and spin 'em in the air just like a whirlwind; they thought they was in a whirlwind. I'm telling you I had quite a life.

Now a lot of my sisters and brothers wanna know, they might wanna know where were we when all this was goin' on. You got to remember that my mother had two sets of children; the first set stopped at Lorena and the other set started at Olivia and took it from Olivia on. An' Olivia might be able to remember some of this, but she's not that old, I'ma tell her she just . . . , I want to make her feel good; she just like the baby of the family compared to . . . I'ma name the first oldest children; there's LV (which is dead), Roosevelt (that's me), Johnny (which is dead), Willie Mae (which is deceased) and then Lorena; that's five right there. Now if you want to get really technical and break it half way, Olivia was like the baby during this time, she was . . . that was six.

That's quite a story. One day I was chopping wood and Olivia was standing out there, she got too close to me, almost scared me to death!! I came down with that axe, I split her face wide open, I hit her in the face with the axe, split it wide open and God blessed that young lady; if it had've been . . . , went one inch deeper, the girl woulda been history. I don't know if she even remembers that or not but it really actually happened. God has certainly blessed us.

LIVING IN THE BOONIES

At one time we were living right there on the freeway . . . , on the highway almost to Daleville uh . . . , uh . . . cemetery, Daleville church, but not down below Mr. Cannon where we lived out in that that field in, out in that pasture, in that big house; they call it Mae Lizzie's house. My brother was coming home from the new ground and something got after him. He ran home, he beat the thing, outran it and got home, that was my brother Johnny. We called the white folks and they got dogs and things, they saw the tracks, they . . . , they was thinking that it was a bear; but we never did catch the animal. That was right next to a half a block from the woods, that's where we lived. Every night we had to go and get our cows and get our hogs and feed 'em. I would go out in the woods and get the rich lighter to burn that green wood, go and cut that green wood, bring it in and make it burn. I'm here to tell you that God has certainly blessed us.

The life that we lived . . . , we would go hunting and that day if we didn't kill a rabbit or some squirrels, we didn't eat. We went and bought our shells, we couldn't just take a practice shot at a rabbit. When the dog would be running'im, he come close to us, we had to make sure that it was a sure shot, we couldn't miss him, 'cause that was a meal. Normally, a rabbit would be hopping slow and when, if he stop, we would blow him away. We see a squirrel up a tree, when he turn around our side; we shoot 'im, that's the way we lived, a lot of days. Then we'd go fishing and sometimes if we didn't catch no fish, we didn't have no meal; that's the way life was with us but a lot of my sisters and brothers don't remember this.

THINGS THAT HAPPENED IN THE "BIG" HOUSE

One thing about it, the black girls had it kinda rough back there. Some of those families had some young ladies, about seventeen and eighteen years old they were beautiful young girls. Really sexy looking, clean looking, developed they would have to go to the white people house and wash the clothes for the white folk. The white ladies would be so busy, they were like secretaries and things and the husband was there at home taking care of the farm and taking care of the people that was working on the farm. So the girls would, the young ladies would cook dinner; wash the clothes and the white women would come in, in the evening time after their work shift was over and the black girls would fix their food, clean up the kitchen, do the washing and go home and come back the next day. But many times while the white woman was away, the white men would rape those young black girls and tell them if they tell their fathers, they gon' beat them to death-lynch 'em and a lot of the fathers got beat like that, some got killed.

Now the school I went to . . . , I'ma call the name of the school 'cause some of you that read my book or hear this tape you gon' know 'bout this school. In fact I have a . . . , my sister married into a family, real light skinned people, my sister Willie Mae married Willie Frank Grady. His family was mixed folk, white people and if my nieces read my book or listen to this tape, they will know that I'm telling the truth. I went to that school and I graduated at Whisenton High there in De Kalb. Looked like more than half of the students there was mixed, beautiful black folk, half white, light brown, they was mixed because of that kinda condition (being raped by the white man), but whenever a girl would get pregnant by these white men, normally what they would do was, they send them out of town and let 'em have the baby.

But listen at this; this is my favorite song playing in the back-ground. I have to keep telling you this, 'bout my favorite song, playing in the back-ground. When I first came to California I went around to my cousin Cobie's house and I listened to these two songs, "Leave it in the Hands of the Lord." And "Someone Watches Over Me". I learned these two songs, and these songs got to be a standard for me. I sang these songs throughout the city. And when I sang, I had people falling out by the score, break up any church, they were shouting all over the churches. I can sing it now, I can still sing. I used to travel all over the city with Larry Jones and the sanctified guitar. I'm gonna put one of my songs on this tape at the very end; I want you all to hear me sing, God anointed me to sing the gospel songs.

Back to these white people. Now, and that's one way that the white people and the black people got a chance to be mixed up; but the white people just didn't like the mixed folk. They treated them, look like, worse than they treated the darker folk for some reason. And some of those mixed folk, look like they had a chip on their shoulder 'cause they were light skinned and they didn't want to talk to the darker skinned people. There were a couple families we knew real good; these folk were real . . . white people. An' I'm gonna say something now; I got some white folks in my family. My grandmother, Pigeon Cole's sister, all of her kids were some of the prettiest children you want to see in your life, they was all mixed up; Aunt Dovey's kids. They were some beautiful folks and some of them live here in California, go to West Angeles Church of God in Christ, and they are beautiful light skinned folk.

One thing about it, we couldn't touch the white people then, when you go back there now and see white folk and black folks, white man and black woman, black man and white woman walking together as husband and wife, it's kinda scary situation but it can be done, now. Ah . . . , you take me for an instance; I never really wanted to touch a white woman, those people, when I was growing up, put something down in me, I've been in California over forty-five years going on and never touched not a one, never touched a white woman in my life and I don't care to touch them. 'Cause they made a god out of them and made us recognize them as such. I said if anything that precious I don't want no part of it. I love my black queen, she's one of the prettiest things that I ever seen, especially since when they done got all mixed up with them other folk. Sometimes you go back to Mississippi, now you don't know who you looking at. You kinda like confused, like a blind dog in a meat house, they are so beautiful, so mixed up.

Quite a story isn't it!! I'm so excited just to be alive to be able to put this tape and book together.

GETTING MY EDUCATION
IN THE SOUTH

There's a song playing in the back-ground, "Steal Away". When I was in Mississippi, I didn't have to steal away, I just prayed and cried and prayed and cried, all day long an' half of the night because of the condition that I was under. I wanted to . . . graduate and go to the big cities and the bright lights to be somebody 'cause when I was graduating, they had a "Who's Who" program and they read my little lines, they said, "They were walking down the streets in Los Angeles, California and they saw a very familiar looking face and as they got close to me an' recognized me from a close-up, they saw it was a classmate, the one and only Roosevelt Leggette." Now that . . . , that meant a lot to me, you see, the white people went to my Dad and told him that I had no business going to school wearing starched and ironed white shirts, that I should be out there in the woods cutting those logs, helping him support that big family. I mean, they stayed on him and my Dad went to my mother and said, "Well, we gon' hafta take Rosey outta school 'cause the white people don't like it cause he goin' to school, say he should be going to work like all the other black boys in the community, to help me with the family." My mother looked at my Dad and said, "Not so!! That boy love school.

I want my children to grow up and be somebody." She said, "Do you not know Jodie, that the only way this boy can be something . . . , he hafta get an education. These white people wouldn't let us get an education here, but we gon' let him at least graduate." She said, "Jodie do you not know that all the books they bring home, some of our kids have seven or eight books or more, an' the books that they bring home are hand-me-down books, the books that the white folk used. The white folks got the brand new books an' they give us the old books." She said, "Do you understand that that boy got books that sometimes he can't even get his lesson out of it 'cause some of the pages are missing. So that mean they put him at the bottom of the pile. She said but if he wanna be something . . . , if I tell him he can't go to school, he cry like a baby an' I'm not gon' stop him, long as he wanna go to school I'm gon' let him go to school and finish school and be somebody."

And do you not know that, in the midst of it all, I went to high school and I graduated. When those white people found out that I had finished school, they congratulated me all over the community. They came to me and asked me to help them figure up the payroll for the people that was picking cotton. The news had gotten out that I was a smart young man. I could add up the cotton and also I could figure out how much they owe the people; so they had me helping them do the payroll. I can remember it as if it was yesterday; this white man asked me, he said, "Little Jodie, Mary Ann picked one hundred and twenty-five pounds of cotton this morning, and she picked two hundred fifty pounds this evening, how many pounds is that. I said well it's not hard to figure up. I said one hundred twenty-five and two hundred fifty, that will give us three hundred and seventy-five pounds. He said, Well Little Jodie, we gon' pay her a dollar a hundred for the cotton that she picked. How much money do we owe her?. I said, "Well; you paying her a dollar a hundred, that a penny a pound. She picked three hundred and seventy-five pounds of cotton, that means you owe her three dollars and seventy-five cents. He thanked me very kindly for that and he congratulated me and he told my mother; he said, "He's a smart young man, we're glad that you let him go on and graduate so he could make something outta himself."

Black people, young people don't let nobody hold you back, these white people didn't hold me back and after I finished, I was 'bout the only black boy in my community that finished high school. An' I was the only one that they would look up to like that. They gave me all kinda respect everywhere I went there. Not only did they give me respect, but all the black boys out in the woods that was cutting logs and the paper wood, they looked up to me. We had one young man in particular, he thought I was a professor, he waited until I had gotten grown and out here in California for about, uh . . . forty years then he told me how he used to look up to me. I really didn't know that but it made me feel good to know that somebody was watching my life. Young people, whatever you do . . . , whatever you do; finish high school. If any way possible, finish college because that's your life, that's your life.!

I'm blessed; I came to California and got a good job, for forty-five years making good money simply because I finished high school. Thank God for my mother!! What if she hadna' stopped my Daddy from letting me go to school. Huh? All I wanted to do was finish high school, I finished high school and God blessed me in a marvelous way to take care of my brothers, my sisters, get them all out here in California. An' my mother and my Dad, my grandmother and I even had my Dad's sister out here and her whole family; the Lord blessed us like that. But it takes education to get out there and dig up that gold, it's there, it's a gold mine there but you got to be educated to dig it up. If you black, you' got nine hundred strikes against you before you even walk outta your front door. So that's why you got to have all the tools that it takes to make it.

VISITING BACK IN MISSISSIPPI

I went to Mississippi an' I drove a brand new Cadillac there. Then we stopped, when we got into the state of Mississippi to get something to eat, at one of those . . . uh, restaurants. We pulled up to the restaurant and I stopped the car on the outside an' my mother said, "Look how those people looking at us. Maybe we shouldn't oughta stop here." I got out of the car, (it was a brand new Cadillac and wouldn't nothing wrong with it) but I had to try to make out some kinda alibi. I raised the hood up, I looked under the hood, then I let the hood down; then we went on to the next place.

And then we stopped and got some food; but I told my mother, "when you go in, order your food first then use the bathroom last," but some did not order the food all at one time. For that cause, some food came out early than the other but they held all the food there and gave it all to us at one time. My mother said to the white lady, she said," My food is cold" But the white lady said, "I can't help it because your food is cold, some of y'all ordered your food at one time and others ordered at another time, that's why it's cold." I tried to give my mother the hint, I even said, "mother," to let her know that . . . , just don't say nothing. That was a smart remark that the white lady had made to my mother.

So after we finished the food, we went on downtown. After we got downtown, we went in one of those five and dime stores; I wanted my kids to see what it was like down there in Mississippi. We went in the five and dime store and on the way out of the store, they had a place where you go to the restroom and they had a water fountain there. My kids stopped and drank water, my second oldest daughter Grace was drinking and a little white girl said, "I want some water." She was so low she couldn't reach the water so Grace reached down and picked the little white girl up and was holding her, letting her drink some water and the little white girl's mother came and snatched her child out of Grace's arms and said, "She don't need no water, she don't <u>want</u> no water!" Grace was saying, "Oh yeah, yeah, she wants some water, she said she wanted some water." Grace was making a big thing out of it. I walked over I said, "Come on baby don't, don't, Hey come on let's go, don't worry 'bout it." My baby was . . . , she was crying it hurt her feelings so bad 'cause out here in California we don't do that kinda crazy prejudice stuff. So . . . , she was hurt, her feelings was hurt.

Then we went on down, went on outside to another store; I had a little ole uh . . . , movie camera with me and they was having a big commotion at this store. What happened was, someone had slapped a black girl and the black people was picketing this store and I was just filming everything being nice and quiet and easy because I was in Mississippi; I know what it's like. There was this big fat white policeman was there looking at me, he didn't say nothing, every move I made he was following me real slowly. I carefully moved around wherever I had to go and I was getting my shots. I didn't, I didn't stir up no kinda anger or nothing, I did it a most professionally way, nice way; getting along with them 'cause I was way down there and I didn't want no problem outta them. So everything worked out all right.

I like to say this to you young people that are in college getting ready to make a career out of your life. Don't mess up your life too early, when you finish college and you know you ready for a career, get married but make sure you marry someone like you that have an education, and make sure that they are saved and filled with the Holy Ghost because even some of these people talking 'bout they're holy you can't hardly make it with 'em. You make sure they sure they got it. Make sure you hear them speak in tongues, make sure you watch their life, make sure you know and see that they walk like Jesus Christ. Then teach her how to pay the bills, how to take care of business around the house and if she doesn't have it already, teach it to her and don't fuss at her if she make a mistake or he make a mistake, we all are entitled to mistakes. I . . . , I taught my wife (she don't like me to say this-<u>no he didn't</u>) by letting her do it. She go out 'an pay the bills, take care of the business an' I just go out and dig up the gold and bring it to her and she put it in the right places.

Make sure these people know how to cook 'cause that's another way of your life 'cause these people in California don't know nothing 'bout cooking. They all say they can cook but nobody will volunteer, but you make sure that they can cook and try to get somebody that love to cook. Don't make no difference how big she get, because you gon' need this brother; out here in this California; 'cause these people don't, they all eat this fast food stuff and that's not good for you. I want you to know that I'm living this life to be an example for my brothers, my sisters and my children. Because . . . , Uh . . . , I had it hard, you don't have to have it hard; my dad had it hard, my mother, my aunties, my uncles, my grand daddies; they had it real hard, you don't have to have like that simply because you have everything to work with.

MY CHILDREN;
MY GREATEST BLESSINGS

I'm so glad the Lord blessed me to raise five beautiful young children. My oldest daughter is **Gretchen** (I'm gonna say) Leggette-Neuble.

This young lady went to college so much, she finished high school and went to college; I asked her, I say, "Honey, what are you gon' do?

What, what, what are you gonna be when you finish college? You goin' to school so much, you goin' more than any child I have." She said, "Daddy, I'm just gonna be a professional student." And I'm here to tell you that she's a smart professional student. She got her first experience, she got her first house, she learned how to pay bills and the young lady got a business job that she was over a record label, she travelled all over the world, even she went to Memphis, Tennessee; she got us a hotel, she got us a rental car she got all the celebrities hotels and rental cars. She just travelled everywhere and she was blessed to marry a young man that's in the church; Church of God in Christ like she was in the church and he has a profession and he travelled all over the world. An' they have two of the most beautiful young people, a young son and a young daughter.

Second: Grace A. Leggette

You take Grace, she in the service, a career lady, very smart. When she was growing up in high school, grade school and in high school, she was a straight "A" student and I wanted Grace to go to college and get a profession and pursue something else but Grace went into the service and she finished college a smart way, through the military; and the Lord blessed her with two beautiful young ladies, young daughters, which they stay with me now and they take care of me too. They are some beautiful young ladies and they both are in college. Isn't that the way to raise your children. Okay that's Grace. Now I had a chance to travel all over the world, part of the world going to see Grace, I went to Hawaii then I flew to England and also to Virginia and many other places just to see Grace. I was blessed to see the parts of world because Grace was there in the military and she's a very smart young lady. She's getting out of the service this year and she's going to retire and she's coming home and she's going to take care of the family here, especially me. My health began to go down now and she's going to come and bless me. I certainly appreciate that. I am godly proud of her, that's the second oldest.

Oldest Son: Grant E. Leggette

You take Grant, he always was a smart young man. In high school he was always busy around home doing stuff, throwing papers, cutting lawns. Grant did many different things to make money and I knew from that he was going to be a smart young man. This young man went to service to pursue a military career fixing planes. When he got out of the service he picked that trade up and made a fortune out of it. As of now he worked in New York for about nine or ten years. He was so good there they flew him here and let him work on planes here at LAX. They liked Grant so well for the way he was fixing planes that they tried to get him to stay several times but he wouldn't stay.

Finally he met a young lady by the name of Betty, a beautiful young lady, she hooked him. He was in New York and he got married here. So he decided he would just come on and work here and be with Betty. The family loves Betty, she is such a sweetheart, she's a jewel. She is real special in this family. We keep trying to tell her that but she really don't know how much we love and appreciate her. She treats me for some reason, I don't know why, she treats me like I'm her real father. I don't want her to ever do any different because it makes you feel good when you know that somebody looks up to you and shows special love. This young lady when she first got married to my son, my car broke down and this young lady let me have her car; go all the way from Riverside to Carson and back every day. I mean she didn't know me. And y'all come talk about how can you not love somebody like that? Don't you say nothing 'bout Betty. I'll get all into your stuff because she's real special, I love my people. Now Grant was one that always has had a business mind about himself. This young man would fly us all over the world. He's already done it. He flew us to Chicago, Memphis Tennessee, Mississippi. All over, everywhere, you name it Grant did it. Hawaii, London England, all these places and we get a chance to sit in first class. All we have to do was pay the taxes. We don't have to worry about paying all that money, just because of Grant. Who cannot be godly proud of a son like that? He's a very smart young man. All we got to do is call him up and he will get us a ticket anywhere we want to go just like that. And as long as Grant's doing that, God is going to always bless him.

If you obey your mother and father and show love to them you will live longer. The Lord thy God will give you some lengthier days, let you live longer. He doesn't only do that for me, he'll do it for all of the members of the family. He did it for my pastor, Elder Jones. Elder Jones was going to Memphis, Tennessee, sitting in coach. Grant was working on the plane and he saw Elder Jones sitting in coach and he walked out and upgraded Elder Jones and put him in first class. That's the kind of young man Grant is. He is always going to be blessed. That's the way you have to be in order to let the Lord bless you.

Youngest Daughter: Griselda Webster

Take my baby daughter, Griselda. Everybody say she's the spoiled one but she is not, she's just the last one. She just a sweet kid, she's very smart in school. She's a real sensitive kid. She's more sensitive than practically all my kid's put together. She's just like a tape recorder, you have to be careful because she's sensitive and she's smart. All those sensitive people are smart anyway. She works for the county and she's a very outstanding worker there. She told them about how long her Dad had been working on his job, how long her mother had been working on her job. When they heard forty-five years on my job and twenty-five years on my wife job, they hired her right up front without any question. She makes top dollars, she makes good money. And she has one of the most beautiful young daughters that you want to see. I call her Daddy's baby, all of my grand kids are my babies. And she comes over and takes care of me. She's eight years old but she takes care of me and I'm godly proud of her.

Youngest Son: Quintin Leggette

Now you take the last one there, Quintin. Quintin has a family. When Quintin was coming up he was so different. He was different from all the children that we had. Quintin was very intelligent, he's smart now but I think he's about half as smart now as he was when he was coming up. Quintin before he got into his grade school, he would ride down the freeway with us in the car with us and he would read the signs up and down the freeway. There were some big letters and he was pronouncing them like a high school student. I knew he was going to be smart. He didn't go to the service, he was smart, he didn't want to go to the service, he wanted to do something else.

I was hoping that he would be an athlete because he could play ball. He graduated out here in Riverside and he went to Chaffey College. I went to see him play football and I thought for sure he was going all the way with football, baseball or something. He hasn't made it there yet. Quintin is an iron-worker, he worked on the 5 freeway, the 91 freeway, the 110 freeway, all these freeways around here. Quintin made extra money because he was working on the freeway, his job title was rod buster. He worked out in Las Vegas and right now he's working out in Perris. He's a hard worker. God has blessed us to have all my children working doing some kind of work and it's all good work because all my children graduated here in Riverside with honors.

When we were in Compton the school district got so bad, so we left Compton and we came to Riverside. They all graduated with honors and they had their chance to do stuff in the schools, in the city out here as a black child. Quintin was playing baseball in the little league, he and Grant and they would sometimes be the only blacks on the team, maybe two other blacks. When Quintin would get up to bat he would hit the ball out of the park and the opposite team would get so upset about that. Gretchen and Grace were the first black cheerleaders on the squad and we were godly proud of them.

Then you take Marie, that's the grand baby, she takes after her mother, she got to be a cheerleader here. We were blessed to have my job to sponsor her to go all the way to Las Vegas, they went there and won the championship and then they went all the way to Florida and my job sponsored them, my job gave them eight hundred dollars just to go all the way to Florida and that's the grand baby. That lets you know if the older ones do good then the last ones will do good.

Thank you very kindly and I hope you will get something out of this story and be able to write something. Put something down on tape for yourself. You, put something down on a tape. Let the folks know when you leave this planet what you've done. A lot of people won't never know. When Jesus got ready to leave this planet and when he left, the stuff he did was recorded. A lot of stuff that we're going by, with the old patriarchs, is something that got recorded, what they've done when they were here. Don't just pass through this planet and don't have nothing left here on record. Let something be left so that people can go by your in life. That's why I'm putting all this down, you haven't heard nothing yet. Thank you very kindly, I will put something else on this.

FEAR, FURY & MY FATHER'S FIST—

W e had a good friend of mine. I went to church with him, I went to school with him. He was a very intelligent young man, he spoke real nice. He was living on this white man's' farm. This White man was named Mr. Leighton. I don't know what happened, but something happened on this farm 'cause this white man shot this young man with a shotgun. Oh my God! His father was out in the field hoeing cotton, his father went crazy. Imagine somebody shooting your son with a shotgun? And the only way they could stop this black man from killing this white man because he shot his son, the white people got around this black man and knocked him out. Ain't nothing we could do about it.

I didn't get along with my father simply because he called me my mother's Black Jesus. I want you to know that my dad was so mean when we was growing up young people, he would cuss every word he say, cuss us all out. When he come in the front door we would go out the back. We would go in the woods somewhere, we didn't want to be around him. But young people you still have to respect your mother and dad.

So, Daddy, one day he was farming, I was out in the field that Friday. I was harrowing off the rows so nice and smooth we were running a planter. If you harrowing off the rows level and smooth that makes it easy for the planter. So I could do it better than my oldest brother so he just wanted me to do the haring, dragging off the road real smooth all the time. So this particular Saturday all the young people were going to town. I wanted to go to town. I had worked five long hard days. Just before we left to go to the field, I said dad I want to go to the town to be with the rest of the people in the community. He told me "No you are not going to town, I want you to harrrow for me today". I said, "Let my brother do it because I did it yesterday". My dad got mad with me, knocked me down. He got a little old, (we had what you called a paper-wood saw), they called it puckwood. He hit at me two or three times and some kinda way he missed me. Mother and 'em got between him and me so he didn't hurt me. Young people that is the kind of environment I was brought up. But I want you to know one thing, you have to treat your mother and father right. If you don't treat them right the Bible says a disobedient child won't live half of his days.

SHOPPING IN TOWN

One day I went to Daleville to get groceries. I was riding a big mule by the name of Ole Doc. If you fell off that mule you couldn't get back on him 'cause he was six feet tall. I went to Daleville and I went in this store and got my groceries and I had Ole Doc outside tied to a tree. Because there was a dark black cloud come over the tree tops rolling, trees popping, thundering, and lightning and raining hard, I was going to wait until the storm passed over before I would try to make my journey back home because I had about ten miles to go. There was a white man there in the store who was going with this store man's wife. The store man wasn't there this day. The store man's name was Mr. Leroy, his wife was Miss Gussie and the man who was going with Miss Gussie was named Buck Moses. He told me, "Little Jodie you better high tail it outta here 'cause a big storm is coming. You better high tail it outta here so you won't be caught in the storm".

I climbed up on that tall mule and I was going down the highway fast as I could trying to beat the storm. When I got about two miles away from that store I had about eight miles to go. The storm hit like a tornado twister wind blowing. There I was stuck out in the storm, blowing so hard, raining so hard the mule couldn't even walk. He just stood still. I laid on all my groceries and put both arms around the mule's neck. Little by little we made it on home. I'm here to tell you I had it hard. I had it so hard. Coming on up through the years, certainly I had it so hard. But I thank God for Jesus, God been good to me. I will continue the rest of my story in a few days, thank you.

How long has it been since you talked to the Lord? The reason why you hear me crying through this story is because I have my mother and father, two brothers and two sisters, grandmother, grand daddy and I have five grand aunties that have gone to be with the Lord. When I start talking about these stories they all come before me as plain as day. My oldest brother was one that my dad didn't give him money like you should give a young man. I don't remember my dad giving me as much as twenty dollars the whole twenty-two years I was home with them, not one time. So my brother would go out and steal money out of the mailbox. He went and stole some money out of a mailbox once and you know any of the neighbors if they see you do something they would tell your mother and your daddy and they wouldn't even question it. They would just beat you. My dad beat my brother so until the clothes stuck to his back, he used the bathroom on his self. My mother tried to stop him but it looked like he was trying to kill my brother.

That put something down in my brother he just didn't want to be home anymore. When he got big enough to take care of his own self, he left home at an early age. That's why everything fell on me. Then I had to be the most dependable child in the family. That's why young people, my brothers and my sisters, I could remember so much 'cause everything fell on me. When everything falls on you sometimes it looks like it is not fair but somebody has to do the chores around home. So, that so far was me. I didn't want that to happen to me but it happened.

GRANDMA'S HANDS—THE SAVING GRACE OF LOVE

You know I can just really remember my grandmother. After I didn't get that red bicycle, when I got about twenty-one years old I went and bought me one. But right now I'm not interested in riding a bike anymore because I'm too big. But one day I was riding my bike, my grandmother would do everything we do. She could ride a bike, play ball, whatever we do she could do it. She was about four feet something tall. She looked like a little kid; she acted like a little kid.

My grandmother had just gotten out of the hospital. I mean she had just had a serious operation. That was about the fourth or fifth operation that she'd had. Then I asked, "Grandmother you want to ride"? She said, "yeah." I set my grandmother up on the handle bars of the bike and I went down the hill. I don't know why I chose to go down that steep hill. We were cruising and she was laughing like a little kid and she stuck her foot in the spokes of the front wheel. Oh my gracious, it scares me now! We went flying through the air like a bird, it tore up the front end of my bike. I grabbed her, scared me to death. I said, "Mama are you hurt"? She said, "No. I'm sorry I tore up your bike." I said, "Don't worry about the bike". I was afraid to go back home because I know mother's going to kill me. But that's the kind of life we lived back in the country. But it didn't hurt her, thank God. She walked away from that. We didn't tell my mother and them about that for a long time. Every time, when she got well, every time I go to tell mother about it she laughs so much, I couldn't tell her. So everything came out O.K.

My dearly beloved, a country life is not an easy life. Everywhere we had to go we had to travel by wagon. We had to go to church in a wagon. But my oldest brother didn't do me fair, he would drive the wagon until we get almost to church then he would turn it over to me. He would get out and walk because he was embarrassed to let the young ladies see him driving a wagon. But that was the way of life. Everybody traveled that way, by wagon. We went to Blackwater Baptist Church. That's where the first time I saw Dr. Martin Luther King. He used to come out there and preach. Dr. King was a civil rights leader, he was a blessing to all of us. (Break)

The reason I was so close to my mother, I was born an asthmatic. I was a very little, small person all my life. I used to go out and try to play with the kids and I'd run out of breath. Then I'd go and lay on my mother's lap until the spell passed over. So that made me kind of special to my mother, I got that extra love that the others didn't get. So when my mother passed away it must have been harder for me than the rest of them. That's why it was so easy for me to do nice things for my mother because she always showed me that special love. Not that she loved me more than she loved the rest of the kids. It was just simply that she was there for me when I needed her.

So now back to the wagon story. My mother's oldest sister's daughter had a little baby girl and they was going to the field one day to do some work. The baby fell out of the wagon, the wagon ran over her and killed her. The little girl's name was Carrie Belle. She was a very pretty young girl. That was one of the first deaths we saw in our family. It was really hard to handle, I couldn't hardly handle that because that was our first one I remember. So you see that I have a lot of great memories. Everybody that lived in the country has something that they can tell you about. It's a good thing to have something you can go back and be thankful for. I am thankful now. I hope that all of you that hear this story, you can get something out of it. Ok? Yours truly Brother Leggette.

SINGING GOSPEL MUSIC

I'm so glad that the Lord saved me. If it had not been for Jesus I wonder where would I be, back there in Mississippi. When I was back there in Mississippi, I used to sing with the Southland Gospel Singers. We were a clean group of young men. We would travel all over Mississippi singing. I remember the very first time we went down to broadcast on WMOX in Meridian. Every one gave us so much hope. They bragged on us, how good we sound. They really pushed us on up to the top. By singing on the radio, that got us a lot of engagements, appointments. We had a chance to sing all over Mississippi.

Just before I came out here, I had a (I really wasn't in love with this girl) young lady. I went to De Kalb and met her up there. She was such a nice young lady. She was one of them half white ones. She was so beautiful this young lady and she was just a sweet young lady. Her name was Mary-Alice Mac Shepard. After I got to California I wrote back to her, we were writing to one another on a pretty regular basis. I asked her to marry me, she said she would. I bought her a very expensive engagement ring and I sent it back to her. We were getting ready to set a date, in fact we set a date. But her mother came down with cancer. She asked me if she could wait a little while, see how her mother was going to come out after the operation. So what I did was I said to her I would wait. But in my waiting I got impatient and while I was waiting, I met the wife that I am married to now.

Wife: Marie Leggette

I married her, but you know God always has our life predestinated, planning ahead what He wants to do. I just felt like it was all in the hands of the Lord. So I am still married to my wife now and the ball is yet rolling. God is blessing me and I don't regret it. She is taking care of me now, because right now my health has begun to fail me. For forty-three years this coming March twenty six we've been married and I have been working ever since in good health. But now I let them operate on my eyes with the laser and it didn't come out good, I can't hardly see. But my wife is standing right there by me. Who knows if I had married that other girl, maybe she wouldn't take care of me like this. But I appreciate it, God knows what He's doing.

We are yet in the land of the living. That's why I am so glad that the Lord saved me.

I'd like to say this one thing: it's a good thing to be saved. If God don't do anything else for me He has done a lot already. I believe that the faith I have in God, the Christian that I am, I believe that God is going to deliver me. I am not saying that if He don't he can, I believe it. Because God's minister, God's pastor Ron M. Gibson looked at me and prayed for me many times and said God's going to let me live; I'm not going to die, I'm going to get healed. So I'm God's responsibility. I'm holding God to this simply because He didn't have to tell me this through his minister. His minister said it and I believe God's minister. I have no other choice but to believe him. Because God healed me once from this condition in my eyes and it lasted about thirty some years. Now this is something else that came up, if God did it then I know He can do it again. And I'm waiting on God I have no other choice. I can't get impatient. I'd like to be able to be like I was before. But I believe God is going to make it even better than it was at first. All you that listen to this testimony don't feel sorry for me, pray with me. Believe God. God can do anything but fail. He has already done so many things in my life.

A lot of people want to know why I have so many stories about my mother. She was just basically all I had when I was growing up really. I told you all about my father, my dad treated us so bad until(I just have to stick this in here). I went downtown, I worked for a whole week, I don't know how much I paid for this shot gun. I went downtown and bought me a shotgun. My dad thought I was buying that gun to go hunting, 'cause that was a way of life, we had to go hunt and kill rabbit and squirrel in order to survive during the winter time. But I bought that gun merely to kill my own father. If he had touched my mother . . . , he fussed at her and cussed at her so much

I got tired of that. But if he had touched her any kind of way after I got that shot gun I would have blown him away. That's bad young people but that is what I had in my heart in my mind, I was going to kill him. But I thank God I left home before all that happened.

When my mother called me and told me to send for her, she was tired of my dad. My wife let me send for my mother and that's the only thing that got her away from him. When he (my dad) came out here she treated him like, real special. She didn't treat him bad at all. I don't know how in the world she could do it but she did it. Young people whatever you do, respect your parents. As I before said your days will be longer upon the land which the Lord thy God giveth thee. I had to put that in there, OK? (Playing a song in the background) I want to see how many of my brothers and sisters can remember this song.

MISSISSIPPI SURVIVAL

I am so glad to be able to talk to you again by the way of this tape. A lot of people see people and they never know what they have gone through, what they came from and how they got over. Like the saying is" Many sees but a few knows". I am reminded when I was doing the share cropping with the white people back in the south. We was on a man's place called Mr. Cannon. A big storm came up and we went in for lunch time, twelve o'clock noon. And we was out to the barn where they keep the horses and the cows and the pigs, hogs. And we saw that twister, twisting like a whirlwind, we saw trees flying in the sky, debris. And we was afraid because it was coming in the direction where we was. The white man was living in a big two story house. He told us to stay outside in the barn. That was the way of life anyway the black man had to stay around animals. He said to us, "If the storm comes directly this way, lay down close to the ground, grab a hold to a little tree, you are more safer than I am in that beautiful home". What could we do? What could we say? We had no other choice. For some reason, it was by the grace of God it didn't hit where we was. When it came close to us it skipped and went around another direction. If you ever saw the path of a tornado it looks like a bull dozer have gone through the woods, just uproot the trees by the score. I want to let you know this one thing, if it had of came our direction, laying down holding on to the ground or tree, we wouldn't even have had a prayer. If it had hit his house, he wouldn't have either.

But I want you to know that God knew that this day was coming, that I would be a blessing to many people throughout the world. I am so glad the Lord blessed me to be able to help others. I am reminded of my mother when she went to the store to get shoes for us, she had to take a string and measure it from our big toe to our heels. Because those white folks wouldn't let you try on those shoes, no way. They didn't want the black folks trying on shoes. So many times I had to wear shoes too small, too large because I wasn't able to go downtown with mother. It's kind of hard for her to have that many measurements in her purse for all the kids. But God,! He blessed us to be here today.

I am reminded when I used to go to my grandmother's house, right off the thirty-nine highway to get water. Every morning we had to get up early to go get the water, we had to tote the water. When my grandmother'd see us coming to get the water, she would call us inside. Let us stand around the fire, that old country fire place and warm up before we take our journey back home with the water and she would give us a butter biscuit. She would give us a home-made biscuit with butter in it. That was the best biscuit I ever eaten in my life.

You know out here in California they don't even use bread no more. And I mean to tell you food was a way of life back in the country. Everybody would have breakfast, dinner and supper. But out here they done changed the name around on everything. We used to live in a little old shack house.

But let's go back to Daleville.

COUNTRY COOKING &
THE BLESSING OF BELOVED
UNCLE BONNER

My Uncle Bonner Bell

I had an uncle lived there in Dayville by the name of Uncle Bonner and Aunt Leola. They lived in a little shotgun house, some of you all don't know what a shotgun house is. A shot gun house is;

90

you could stand at the front door, look all the way through out the back door. My Uncle Bonner, he thought the world of me because I was one in that particular community where I was living at, one of the young men that was going to school. But the way of life is that most young men would drop out of school and start cutting logs; paper wood. They never made any thing out of themselves. But my uncle in the midst of all of his children, he would slip me twenty to twenty-five cents almost every week. He was working for the white people there and they would pay him. He always had some money in his pocket. The word is when we wanted something good to eat we would go down to Uncle Bonner's house.

He would barbeque and we would sit up all night long and barbeque with him. Long about midnight or one o'clock in the morning that meat would start cooking, start smelling it was almost done. The foxes start howling, the bobcats start squalling and we sit closely to Uncle Bonner. They wouldn't come close to us but they would come all around. He protected us and Uncle Bonner would raise up the shoulder part of the hog, reach under there and get that lean meat. About now, it's done and he would give all us a piece and we would sit around that fire and eat that barbeque. Those were some good days to us.

But now I don't know how this happened, looked like this man could have lived for ever. This man treated me better than my own father treated me. And he was a mentor for me. I didn't know what that word was then but I know now. He was a mentor, he was one that I looked up to. When I got out here in California he passed away. And when he passed away I had a brand new Cadillac, I just bought it. I saw him when he died *on my screen*. I told my mother to call my first cousin and tell him I saw him, ask was his father sick. He said yeah he was sick but he was getting out real soon, in a few days.

I said tell him that I saw his father pass away, but if he needs my car, I just bought a brand new Cadillac, he could use it to drive home, because if anything happens I'm going to fly. My uncle's sister Hattie Mae passed away and they (his children) went to the hospital, he was sitting on the bed and he was waiting for Aunt Leola to come pick him up. They told him that his sister Hattie Mae passed away. When they told him Hattie Mae passed away, he had a heart attack right there on the bed and died. I caught the plane, went on back to Mississippi. They had both funerals the same day. The Lord showed it to me. I guess God said well since he was so close to you I'm going to go on and let you see ahead of time so you can get ready. Then I went on back, we buried Uncle Bonner, looked like to me that was the worst thing that had happened to me.

GOD'S BROADCAST:
MAKING A JOYFUL NOISE

Then the Lord put on my heart to have a spiritual broadcast. I went on the radio station back there, WMOX. I called up the radio man and told him I wanted to go on a few months. I was planning on just hitting Mississippi—Meridian, maybe one or two months and just travel all over the whole world. Because the Lord gave me this testimony about when I was sick and in the hospital and he raised me up and I wanted to let the world to know about it. I went on the radio and I used Elder Steward's church. Elder Steward's choir would come on singing and bring us on. I would give my testimony and have words to the people there in radio land. Then I would turn it over to Elder Steward and he was one of the most preachingest preachers that you ever want to hear anywhere and he would preach us off the air. We only had a fifteen minute broadcast but that was one of the most powerful broadcast I heard in my life.

Well Brother Leggette why you said the most powerful? Because when we would go off the air there, they would call out here crying and rejoicing and excited about the broadcast. And when I went back to bury my uncle I saw a lot of my friends that lived out in the red hills of Mississippi, out in the country. I was in the church and they was hugging me and shaking my hand and telling me, "Oh that broadcast . . . , that broadcast". I couldn't even have a funeral, I didn't have time to cry. They treated me as thought I was a celebrity. And all I did was have a broadcast and gave it all I had. I had a little twelve year old missionary, little sister Brumfield. I would put her on the air sometimes and they just loved her to death. I called the radio station, I told the man, "I think I have to cancel because I want to hit a few other states before I go off". The radio man said, "No, no you can't do that Mr. Leggette:. He said," Your ratings right here in Meridian is the highest rating that we got on any broadcast we got here, so you can't do it". He said, "We want you to stay on a while longer". I guess I must have been on there about five or six more months then.

We wind up staying over a year on that radio broadcast. I've done what God asked me to do and anything else he wants me to do I am ready to do it. He enhanced my ministry with the video. I traveled all the world out of the United States, traveled to Paris, France; Frankfurt, Germany; East Berlin behind the walls; London, England; Bahamas; Hawaii, Chicago, Mississippi. Many years I went year after year to Memphis Tennessee to tape the holy convocation. I did what the Lord told me to do. Even with my back to the wall I am asking God to give me a little more time. Because there are many people out there dying who don't know God in the pardon of their sins.

My mother, she use to walk miles just to take care of us, wash, iron and do all this stuff and she only was getting like seventy-five cents to a dollar and a quarter a day. I don't know how she made it but it is not for me to know how she made it. It was God that did it. One thing I can say about my mother is the reason she telling us she wanted us to be good students in school, she said that when she was in school she was the head of her class and she wanted us to be that way. I don't know how many of my brothers and sisters graduated in Meridian but I was blessed to graduate only because of my mother. But I'm going to tell what I am going to do, I am going to check with them and see how many of them did.

Well, thank God for mama. You know mamas' is one of the greatest thing that ever been given to the world. Nothing like mama. I was just imagining, just sitting here talking and I can see Mary kneeling at the cross and she looked up at the cross and she looked back at the crowd and she said to the crowd, "That's my son hanging on the cross, he's never done nobody wrong. But he's dying for the whole world, look at him my son". And when Jesus looked at John he said, "John I want you to take care of my mother". He said, "Mother I want you to look unto John, he is going to take care of you". We all are like that.

My grand daddy called me. He said, "Roosevelt I am sick and I'm not going to get well." He said, "I don't want to leave but I got to go". He said, "I want you to make me one promise". [Who-o, glory to God.] "I want you, at my death; I ain't gone be around here long, I want you to send and get your grandmother 'cause she think a lot of you all and I want you to take care of her". He said, "She's hard headed but I want you to send and get her. 'Cause she won't do nothing I tell her she just hard headed. I just hate to leave her.' And I sent and got my grandmother and she stayed out here. And grandmother asked me to make her one promise. She said, "When I die I want you to send my body to Mississippi". Sure enough when my grandmother passed away, (I've done a lot of stuff, I didn't realize how much stuff I've done. I'm almost a very important person, huh?) then I shipped her body back there, we had the funeral. And I buried her right beside Papa, right there in Daleville. But I thank God that he blessed me to do all this. And I believe God is going to Bless me in a most definite way.

And I thank God for this testimony hoping that if it can be used in any kind of a professional level I hope somebody can hear it and decide to treat their mother, father, sister, brother, kids even better than they are doing now. You know that we are not just here by accident, we are here by the grace of God. God didn't have to do it. Because I am talking now putting all this testimony on this video tape I don't see no death in sight for me but I just want to do this just because God is moving on me now to do it. If there ever was a time that we need to do something for the Lord to get busy, the time is now. Because he's not coming until the Gospel has reached the whole entire world. Then I feel like that, he's not coming right away because we got a few more days to go before the Gospel will get around. Thank you very kindly and I'm hoping that you all can get something out of this, this tape, this message.

This is my way of delivering the word throughout the world. Everybody else have a way. God is holding all of us responsible for those that are lost. Whatever kind of way you can reach the lost it's going to be a cost. But God wants us to reach them at any cost, Huh? I want all my cousins to listen to this tape and I know some of you all can remember. Mae can remember a lot, Floyd can remember a lot but I know Sis should be able to remember a little but I don't know if . . . uh if the rest of the kids can remember because they were young. So why would I bring all this stuff up. Simply because when Jesus left, they left his story on record and I want mine left on record. All right?

GOD'S FISHES & LOAVES

I'm so grateful to have this opportunity to put on this tape things that happened to me in California. The Lord blessed me to leave Mississippi in1957. I came to California and I made this my home. This is the month of December right now, 2006. So we are getting ready for the Christmas celebration. In just a few weeks, just three weeks it's going to be Christmas. So we like to go into some of the things I went through since I've been here in this beautiful city of the angels. In coming to California I received a beautiful life from the Lord.

I came here and didn't have a job. I got here like about Saturday by Monday I went out on a job with my homies and the Lord blessed me with a job. Well I was driving the trash truck and in fact I was a helper at that time but as time progressed and I stayed there for a minute and I progressed real fast. I went up in my life, learned how to drive and I was just dumping trash from the streets and I was working real hard. We were working on salary. The quicker we got through the quicker we went home. So the Lord blessed me with a wife in 1959, two years after I came here. And he blessed us with, I don't know what happened, it was like boom, boom, boom, boom, boom, I looked around and I got five children; three beautiful daughters and two sons. And from those five children we have twelve grandchildren now. And it's been like almost forty-eight years since my wife and I have been married now. In March it will be forty-eight years.

So I went and got this job in Gardena when I first got here, working with the Municipal Service Company. I had some good friends, good workers that was working, who taught me how to do it all because coming here out of Mississippi I didn't know anything about that type of work but they taught me how to do it. And the boss loved my work so much after the first day he hired me right on the spot. And I stayed there for nine long years. And things were kind of hard for me because my mother and father was disabled and living in Mississippi. And I was the only one that had income coming in. So I would send them twenty-five dollars a week back home and I had twenty-five dollars to live on and pay my rent room and board for Olivia and I. So once I did that I didn't have enough money left to buy lunch, to buy my gas going to work and back with my friends. They would charge me just so much, maybe a dollar a day or something. But I didn't have that; so it might sound a little sad to you but God brought me from a mighty long way. What I would do was I would save bottles. Coke bottles, beer bottles, water bottles, every kind of bottle that I could. We had a water bottle that if you turned it in you get ten cents for it and had another bottle, Mother's Pride, that if you turned it in you get ten cents for that and the big beer bottles you would get five cents and the soda bottles five cents. So I saved enough bottles in the run of the day, I was able to eat everyday by saving bottles 'cause that's all I had. I couldn't go out to the movies with the girls and enjoy life like other guy's did simply because I was sending my money home to mother and all those children.

It was twelve of us and when I left there, I left ten there and then nobody working. And my responsibility was, I felt, to take care of mother and dad. So I worked there all of those years and I learned to how to drive the truck. Those Mexicans treated us real bad, 'cause they was prejudiced, they treated us real bad but some kind of way I made it, the Lord blessed me to make it. The boss, the supervisor was a Mexican and he liked me simply because I would do what he told me to do. But he never did understand my Christian life, 'cause he was an atheist. But something about his family, he would take up for his family and by him taking up for his family that made it rough and bad for us because we had to take the seconds in everything and they had first. They would work us real hard and they would take the easy routes and make us do the hard routes.

So now I had a family and when it came Christmas time I didn't have the money to buy toys and buy goods and buy presents. But the job route that I was working on was a lot of Japanese. They would come out and give you two dollars and three dollars at this stop, a box of candy at the next. They would give us so much stuff that about two weeks during the Christmas rush a week before Christmas and a week after Christmas they would give us so much money and candies and gifts until I had enough for my family. Every day I went home I had a box full of goodies for my family. And one day, I can remember this just as plain as day, look like I will never forget this, money was really a problem; five children, trying to pay a house payment, car payment out of a hundred and two dollars a week. I had worked there nine years and the most that I had ever made in that ninth year, that was when I got my highest raise was a hundred and two dollars. So what I did was I was working out in the streets and the mailman came by and he was driving kind of fast and he turned the corner and something fell from his truck. And I saw the package and I had wanted to get my wife something for Christmas but I didn't have the money. So I ran, picked the package up and I'm hoping to stop him but he got out of sight real fast. So I took it home, it was a brand new dress, the size of my wife and I gave her that for Christmas. Thank God for how He brought me through many different things.

FAITH, VISION & TIMING: QUICK ACTION BRINGS ADVANCEMENT

One day I was working, this is what made the boss really like me, I was working and his brother was the driver and I was the helper. His brother got sick and we had to take the truck to the yard. I didn't know how to drive it so what his brother did was, his brother would shift the gears for me and I steered the truck directly all the way to the yard and then the boss saw me pull up in the yard and he came out to see what was wrong. I told him his brother was sick and I brought the truck home safely, no accidents, no nothing. From that point on he made me something like his foreman and every time he needed something really important he would give it to me.

I wanted to get me a Cadillac and every time I needed money I would go to the big boss who was Armenian and he was one of those guys who knew I was a Christian and he called me his deacon. I would go to his house and take my kids and let them meet him and he just like fell in love with me. I was a Sunday school man and he was really good on the bible, one of those Armenians that really knew the bible. So this man would help me get my Sunday school lesson together. Then I told him I said, "You know I like that Cadillac you got. One of these days I'm going to get me a Cadillac". He said,

"Go out and find you one and I'll loan you the money to pay for it". I went out and found myself a Cadillac. He loaned me the money to pay for it and he took out so much a week, like maybe four or five dollars a week until I paid him. I'm the only one on the job that had a good car all the time and all of the rest of them didn't know how I was getting the money because they knew I wasn't making very much money there. So I got a used one, not a new one but I got my Cadillac, the Lord blessed me.

So I was working so hard and I said it looked like someone would see me working and say they would offer me a good job. One day the big boss pulled up behind me, I saw his Cadillac turn the corner. When I saw that I started working real hard. He pulled up behind and followed me for about a block. Then I acted like I didn't see him. I was just throwing those cans. Then all of a sudden he blew his horn. I run back there and it was him. I shook his hand like I didn't know he was back there, but I knew he was back there all the time. He was telling me what a good worker I was and if everyone would work like me and stop complaining about wanting more money the job would even be easier for everybody.

When I got ready to leave the job, it was hard for me to leave that job but I had to advance myself some kind of way 'cause I wasn't going nowhere, just staying in the same little old rut. We was picking up those fifty-five gallon barrels and throwing them on top of the truck and all that kind of stuff, it was really hard. So on my way home I had a brother-n-law, Elder Ash. He came to California and I got him a job with me but he quit the job and went on and got a job at another place. I asked Elder Ash to look out for me. He told me where this new job was, told me to go by and put in an application. I went by and put in an application and the man said, "You know, do you really know somebody who wants to work?" I said I couldn't think of nobody else. Then he said, "Fill the application out. I'll call you if I need you". When I got home that evening, he called me. He said, "Well I got a job for you. If you know someone who wants to work I got a job". I said, "Well yeah, I'll work it."

I didn't give my old boss not one day's notice. What I did was, the new guy told me to come to work that next morning. And he told me who to go out with another driver. I went out before day in the morning and I went out with the guy and I liked the job. I was very smart. He was just going around in circles, so I took his route book and I routed it in a way where he could start out at one end and end up at the other end and it was much easier for him and me both. It cut his job by like two hours and he wouldn't have to be back tracking. So the boss saw that I was a smart man. So they taught me how to drive the truck good there. I got my license and then I got my own route and I was off and running—I was going.

The Power of Tithing: Union
Organizing & Prosperity.

What happened now; it was a non-union job. I worked there for about three or four years. I brought the union in and signed everybody up. And then the big boss got upset with me because I signed them all up because he didn't want the union on the job. I signed them up and once they signed up that was history. Then one of the black guys went and snitched on me to the boss and told him I was the one behind it and he tried to get me fired. But I was such a good worker, I did so much work for the company and all the customers liked me. So he kinda like forgot about it and then from that point on we got to be a union job.

First I was making like about a hundred and thirty dollars a week. I went from a hundred and thirty dollars with the union and on the clock to about two hundred a week, then to three hundred, four hundred, five hundred. Then I quit that job when I was disabled with my sight I quit that job about six years ago. The job called for about six days work an' I worked that job for about thirty years for six days a week, then I started working five days. I was making more in five days than I was at six because I had got my raises and I had advanced myself in the union. So what I did was I was making twelve hundred dollars a week after we got all the raises.

So when I made twelve hundred dollars a week they would take out so much, couple of hundred dollars. So I asked my supervisor to please let me work five days. Then I was working five days and I was making about nine fifty but I was taking home more for nine fifty than I was when I was working the whole six day. So I had the Mexicans to work in my place and they really loved working in my place making all that extra money. They had a house full of kids and all of my kids was gone.

So what happened was I started working in the city of Inglewood and all the customers liked me so well. The big boss said we lost our contract and I had a city worker, a lady who worked for the city and she told her husband. I went to his house to pick his trash up and he liked me real well and we were just talking, and I told him that we had lost the contract. He said, "My wife works for the city; she says if you get letters from the people and give it to the city they will give you that contract back." Now there was a lady that was working in the city, what she did was she drafted a letter, it was a beautiful letter. She said, "You have them handwrite a letter something like this. Don't write it exactly the same way but this is something to show you what to do". I took that letter and showed it to my customers and I got about two hundred letters and we turned those letters in to the city councilman and they had a meeting.

And they gave us the contract back although we was under bid. My boss was so excited to get all those thousands of dollars contract back that what he did was he sent my wife and I to Hawaii on a six or seven day vacation paid hotel room and board. He told me to take a vacation 'cause I did so much for the job. I went to Palm Springs, I had a vacation home there. I was going to use my vacation home and take that money that was going to be clear for me. I showed it to him and he said, "Oh Rosy, I want you to take a vacation, that's not a vacation." My wife saw a vacation in the book so she wanted one of those Hawaiian vacations and she said, "Why don't you take this to him and see if he will consider it?" And I said, "Well I don't think he will pay that much". And she said, "Well you have not because you ask not. Just try it." I took it and I gave the vacation thing to the head secretary and I said, "Give this to my boss. Tell him this is the one I want right here". I went back the next day and she said, "He accepts it and he told me to tell you here's a check for you and he was glad to do it." So I went, took the vacation and by now I'm a supervisor, I'm a union steward and I'm really moving now. I got everything in my hand, looking really good now. So we went there and while I was there in Hawaii I took pictures of the Hula girls and they signed it. When I got back they put it on the board and I sent the supervisor something special.

But what happened, some of the other supervisors got mad with me and called me the owner's man, in other words the 'white folks nigger.' Anyway, so they turned against me. We were working at one branch; so the boss wanted to mix all the roll-off together. He took us away from the roll-off in the front loaders and sent me to this branch. This branch is the one that didn't want to let me go on vacation.

What happened, I am a little ahead of myself. First, just before I went on vacation I went to this supervisor, he was the operational manager, "I said I want to take a vacation this month. He said, "You cain't no take a vacation this month simply because what is happening is, we are not giving vacations this month". I said, "Well the big boss wants to give me a vacation". So he said, "Well, OK, if he wants to give you a vacation we have to honor that". So he gave me the vacation time; I went and took the vacation and came back. After that, he did everything in his power to make me quit. He couldn't fire me because the boss told him, "I want you to take care of Rosy. I'm sending him over here with the rest of the drivers but I definitely want you to take care of him." They busted me down from sixty some hours a week down to forty, now I'm not making nothing. I felt so ashamed of giving the Lord tithes out of that forty hours; it wasn't no money just paying tithes on the take home pay.

So what I did I gave the Lord tithes out of the whole amount. When I gave the Lord tithes out of the whole amount, then the Lord blessed me. So I worked there and the boss wanted me to take off and come to all of their meetings and bring my camera and tape the meetings for twelve hours and all I do is tape and eat and they wouldn't let the others go. So that created friction between the drivers, supervisors, and the managers and me. So there I was caught between a rock and a hard place. So I went and bought myself houses. I had a lot of equity in my houses. The Lord had blessed me and my wife to buy ten houses and a big plot of ground since we had been married so I had something to work with. So they cut me down real low. But I went and borrowed some money on my house and went and bought myself a brand new Cadillac off the floor, no miles, brand new Cadillac. And I went to the big celebration. I drove it there, when I got there they got my car, they parked it. And after the taping was all over, I went by the office and I called the young lady, she was the secretary, and I called her out. She was very nice and I said, "I want you to come in here and look at what I got your mother". I called her my daughter so I said, "I want you to meet your mother". So she come out and hugged my wife and she looked at the Cadillac and she loved the Cadillac so much. And while they was hugging each other and talking I went and got the supervisor. I said, "man he loves Cadillacs," his father had one. He come out there and he saw that new Cadillac and he almost went crazy. But he liked the Cadillac, he really did.

Then what happened was I went on back to work. Those people got so upset with me, they took me from one place and put me at another place in the city of Inglewood. Then they took me out of the city of Inglewood and put me in Long Beach. And I was working by commission. If you haul ten or twelve loads that's good money. I could make fourteen, no problem because I was a hustler. That's why the bosses liked me because I was what they called their quota man. So this Armenian guy, was the general manager, took me out of the city and put me in Long Beach. And I was going to work before day in the morning and they was giving me one job. So what I did was after I got that one job, I just drove all over the whole city, praying asking the Lord to make it fertile. After I got through praying over that whole city, this is the God's honest truth, the Lord blessed me with so much work. It took four and five trucks and we still couldn't keep up with it. I am serious. I was making more loads than anybody, they couldn't figure that one out. Then I turned right around and got myself another new Cadillac. Now they are really upset with me. But God blessed me in such a way.

DIVINE PROPHESY: THE DOWNFALL & REMOVAL OF CORRUPT BOSSES.

So I got a call from the office. They said, "Rosy we want you to come to the office". This new company had bought us out and the new general manager was messing with the money, stealing the money. We got cd's; that means we would get four hundred dollars a load and we turn the money in every day and we had a paper that go with it. With all the cash, he was taking the cash and putting it in his pocket. Like three hundred and fifty dollars a box. And he was putting all that cash into his pockets and all he was doing was showing the charge accounts. So they caught up with him. They wanted me to come to the yard, I thought they might have thought I was stealing because I was buying new Cadillacs. So I went to the yard and I said I'll be there tonight then one mind said no you better go now because they might think you taking their money buying new Cadillacs.

I went to the yard, when I got there, there was an investigator there. I didn't know how to talk to him because there was a new company, a new investigator and then my job was at stake. He had a stack of papers about three inches thick. One of the little secretaries I call her my god baby, every time she turned in a paper she would make a copy and keep it for herself. So when all this stuff came down, she sent all this paper work over to the big boss and he started investigating. And one of the guys that was working there with me they got rid of him and he got mad and he had a law suit and he told this investigator to talk with me. I been there longer than anybody and I would tell them everything. But he started talking to me and I didn't know what to say.

Then I said there ain't no sense being a fool the man asked me the question. He's showing me all this paper work. I looked at it and I said, "Well yeah I know about all this I know what's going on. I said, "This Armenian guy is buying new trucks and giving all the new trucks to his people. Going to Hollywood hiring new people and getting rid of all the blacks and the Mexicans. If you don't believe what I'm saying all you got to do is just wait until they come in. They will be come in this evening. Just go to the guard shack and sit there and watch you will see for yourself". He said, "No I don't want to do that. They are paying me so many hundreds of dollars an hour just to do this". He said, "What do you know about this"? When he started asking me questions, I opened up. I told him everything he wanted to know and then some. He went and talked with three more black guys and then he went upstairs. We had a brand new building and this guy had been there for about seventeen or eighteen years as general manager. They cleaned out all of those Armenians, got rid of every one of them.

Now we looking good. They put me in a brand new truck, that brand new truck that one of those Armenians had, they gave it to me. It had a push button, it had hydraulics, everything was push button and computer shift. I was really soaring now. I was making as much money as I wanted. If I want to go out there and make twelve hours a day I would go and make myself twelve hours. If I wanted to go make fourteen, fifteen it didn't matter. They couldn't say nothing because every time you haul a load it takes about an hour to haul a load. And every time you haul a load it was paying the company like three fifty to four hundred dollars. So as long as I stayed out there the more money I made them and they didn't care. And I wasn't making that much, whatever the hourly rate was and they was making twenty times as much as I was making and even more. But anyway the Lord blessed me and I stayed there a little while longer and they got rid of all those people.

DIVINE FAVOR:
VICTORY OVER WORK QUOTAS

N ow the manager that gave me a rough time he had to do what the general manager told him. Now he turned to love me. He done everything he could to help me. He put me in different cities, he made it really nice for me. Right then I would go in his office and pray with him, talk with him and counsel with him. After he did me all like this. So one day he was in his office sitting there and he was just going through all kinds of changes. I said, "What's wrong son"? He said, "The general manager is giving me a problem". I said, "God is going to make a change in this company". That was a little before they got rid of the general manager. I said, "Look I have this thing, I have *this screen* and I see stuff in advance. You don't know what this is but I want to let you know the Lord gave me this gift". He said, "I know what it is, my daddy has this same kind of gift". I said, "Oh yeah, Ok now. I want to tell you this, God is going to make a move on this job in just a few days. If God don't make a move in a few days call me a lying prophet and don't believe nothing else I say". That's when they got rid of the man. From that point on he believed everything I said.

So now we got to a point where they wanted to transfer us back to another branch. At this branch they had a black guy there, he apparently was a mean guy to people. He didn't care about folks. That's what I thought, that's what the Mexicans had told me and I was believing them, so I didn't want to go down there. So they were going to send half of the guys, the ones they didn't want down there with him. And they were going to keep the rest of the good guys up there with us. So that wasn't quite fair. I asked them, "How are you going to pick this thing, are you going to pick it random or are you just going to send the guys that you don't like"? He said, "We are going to do it like this".

The Lord put something in my mind. Spirit said, "Well you have your way with these drivers. They will work for you more than they will work for the general manager here. What I want you to do is get together. Rally around the drivers. Get together with them and tell them that you are going to bust your hide. Everyone is going to haul as many loads as we can haul. And see if that load count will change things.

There was about thirty drivers. So we was averaging about two hundred loads a day. Two hundred loads times three fifty to four hundred dollars, that was good money. So I rallied around with those guys we got together and I told the operational manager, I said, "Let me have my way with these guys, you don't want to get rid of the guys, you want to keep everybody here. You are strong and making your quota. Let me have a meeting with the guys". I had a meeting with the guys and told them, "I am not your supervisor per se but I am the supervisor now. They hired me as a supervisor and I have been working with this operational manager and everything is working out good". I said, "Now what we're going to do is we are going to go out there for this whole week. We're going to bust our suds and what we're going to do is we are going to haul as many loads as we can. Work through your lunch break, I don't care what, work with a sandwich in your hand". They all worked with me. I said, "Now I'm not going down there because I'm one of the older guys. I don't have to go. But some of you guys are new, you don't have a lot of choice". I said, "But what we are going to do is we are going to haul so many loads, we are going to blow their minds".

So we got together and we started working together. Then we hauled three hundred and something loads; from two hundred to three something. That blew their minds. Then the man from the other branch called the general manager and said, "When are you going to send me my drivers"? The general manager said, "Well they are making their quotas, more than making their quotas. I'm going to leave them up here. We are not sending you nobody. You all are not making your quota with what you got and now you want these drivers". The news got back to me. The operational manager said, "Rosy. You know what you did with those guys? Well that worked. I got a call today and the big boss said he don't want the guys down there and he was praising us for all those loads we made. He said we can stay there for as long as we want to stay there".

BOLD FAITH: HANDLING WILDCAT STRIKES & COLLECTIVE BARGAINING

B ut now we had new managers here and they want to change things around. They lost the contract with the union. We had six wildcat strikes and the seventh one I took all the mechanics, everybody who had a driver's license, it didn't have to be a truck driver's license. We drove across that wildcat strike line. I had about ten or twelve guys and we went out and worked all day, some just went around the corner and parked. When we came back it scared those guys so bad 'til everybody went to work. So the boss put his arm around me again 'cause I won that battle.

So anytime the union had a problem the union told me to do it, anytime we drivers had a problem and I call the union, I say I want you to send me out a representative right now. The new big boss wanted to do a whole lot of crazy stuff. So I took the letter heading of the union and put it on another letter and I had every driver sign his name on a big sheet of paper. Then I got some scotch tape and stuck the letter heading on the paper and put it in the Xerox machine and made a copy and it looked legal. Then I gave it to that union representative. He went up and gave the boss one of them.

When I got in that morning I was in the office talking to the new boss. I always stayed busy anyway, I talked business and they didn't play with me and my drivers. No, no because I had the union on my side. So when the general manager came in, someone came to me and told me he was looking for me. They told him I was in the office having a meeting. He said, "Rosy when you get out of the meeting I want to talk to you". After I got out of the meeting he said, "Rosy are you aware of this letter that's around here"? I said, "yeah I'm very much aware of it. I know all about it." He said, "What's going on"? I said, "Well the drivers are not pleased with the way you are doing things around here. Unless you change things around all the guys are threatening to write a letter or call to the head-quarters in Texas." He was a black man and didn't want to lose his job. 'Plus I'm gonna get on a plane and fly down there and I'm gonna talk to them people and let them know what's going on, let 'em know who I am and all. I'll let them know I'm representing the union".

Then he said, "Let's go in my room". I said, "I don't feel comfortable going in your room talking to you, leaving my drivers down here, making it look like it's a put up and you paying me off to do this. But I will go up there with you, but you've got to act right." See he would pray and I would pray. We would get in the office and we hold hands and we would pray. I said, "Now you're a man of God and I'm a man of God when we have problems we pray". I said, "If you don't do what I'm asking you to do now, I'm not trying to make you do nothing. But if you don't do what I am asking you to do now and all those drives are looking for something. All we want you to do is let the drivers come and we have a talk with the drivers one on one and let them tell you how things are going and how displeased they are". He said, "Ok I'll do that". I said, "We don't have a coffee pot, we don't have nothing here. I will talk about this stuff, but a lot of stuff I'm not gonna talk about because my drivers are not here. When we have the meeting, then I'll talk". I started working at six o'clock in the morning and we were talking until about nine. I said, "Man I got to get out of here I have to go and do my route, my customers are waiting for me". He kinda like to hear that. He said, "Well you make more loads than anyone here". I said, "Simply because I'm concerned about my job. I got customers out there and they're gonna be calling after a while. Let me go out there and we will meet together after a while". He said, "Can I meet you on the route"? I said, "No you can't meet me on route, you gonna take up my time. You just do what we asked you on this letter and we won't have no problems." I got in that evening and he had bought us a great big coffee pot, five or ten gallon pot. He got us jackets, he got us caps. He got us stuff that nobody was getting.

IN SICKNESS & IN HEALTH: GRATITUDE IN A SEASON OF CHANGE

When I went to take the laser surgery that messed up my eyes, we didn't have no work for light duty. So that black man, the big boss that all the Mexicans said was so bad, he told me to go down and tell the manager to give me some light duty work to do. I went down there and I said, "You know what, I don't like being down here, I'm not comfortable. My drivers are up there and they are not performing. You got to drive those guys, you got to stay on them. But the manager up there he is easy. But I get on their behinds and make them produce. I want to go back up there". He said, "Rosy, whatever you want to do go ahead". So when I got back up there he said, "Rosy you tell this man I said to give you a job. Just go out there and put sand over the oil that the trucks drop. Then go sit down. If you want to draw disability we need you to stay here for three or four months. All you got to do is sit here". I sat there for about two weeks and I got so bored, I got so tired. I said I really can't do this. I felt like I was taking their money. I would stay there twelve hours a day sixty hours a week, making a good check doing nothing.

So I said, "Boss look, I can't do this. Let me draw my disability. After I draw my disability, if I be well enough, I'll come back". I drew

118

my disability for a whole year and now it's time for me to draw my retirement. So I knew my sight was gone and I couldn't come back. I filled out a letter form for retirement and it took about a year to get retirement. So I called them and asked, "Why don't you guys just turn me a loose so I can get my retirement"? He said, "Rosy you want to draw your retirement"? I said, "yeah". He said, "Well I didn't know ". I said, "I sent the letter in and the lady said you wouldn't sign it". He said, "The reason I wouldn't sign it is we were looking for you to come back". I'm sixty-six years old, can't see and they want me to come back. That's how the Lord blessed me in order to work. I worked every day. Rain or shine, sleet or snow. What I would do is, I worked all my sick days, I was the healthiest on the job. After working my sick days I would save all that money up and give to my kids for Christmas, I gave them all a hundred dollars apiece, all five of them. And then we had money left with my floating holidays, I had enough to do it. So the Lord blessed me. I was never sick for thirty-six years on that one job.

CHURCHES AND INFLUENCE
IN MY LATER LIFE

So, after I moved out here in Riverside and stayed a while, then I start . . . , I went around to Life Church and I joined up with, uh . . . Reverend Gibson. We joined that church and we stayed there for a while, not long, because I was not familiar with the way that he did church work. He was younger and he had young ideas, an' he didn't do things like Elder Jones did it, so that, that threw me off a little bit.

So I was a video man, I put the first camera in his church. When he used to come and preach for me at New Jerusalem on Men's Day, I would sell out tapes, I would sell so many tapes and he saw me selling tapes, taking orders, then that moved on him, then he didn't want me taping at his church, he kinda act like he did but he didn't. So what happened, I start taping and people liked the way I taped because I did it the professional way, I did it professional and I did it right and they liked it. My tapes were goin' an' I told him, look, you don't have to pay me for taping, all I want you to do is just sign my contract, that contract say that I gave this much in tapes and then like that I could have proof so I could claim it at the end of the year on my taxes. So one year I had four or five full pages that I turned in, I showed it to him that I collected money and I gave it all back to his pastor's aid president and they were all excited about that. So I left there and they had me going all over the place taping.

About a year later, we were taping something for the young people. I taped and I was walking around in the hotel in the lobby and they were asking me what did I want for the tapes, how much was I gonna sell them for? I had taped three nights and I said I let you have all three of the tapes for a certain price. It came out real nice and clear. Then what happened, I said, "I want you to make an announcement brother president, let'em know that the tapes will be ready and we're getting ready to go home and if they want tapes, put in their order now then I'll know how many sets to put together." So what happened, when I said that, the president said, "Well I want you to make the announcement, 'cause you got your way with words and you can speak it better than I can." So I got up and testified and let them know that the tapes would be ready, they all came out good, I built the speaker up real good, 'cause he was a great speaker and his wife was great and I said, "This is one of the better recordings that I ever done." The pastor walked over to me and took the mike out of my hand and said Brother Leggette, "Is there anything in this for the church?" And I said, "Every bit of it." So, I had already talked to the pastor's aid president about giving it all back to the church anyway so I could get it claimed for my taxes. Then he said, "Church, this is a good brother," he said, "What I want you to do Brother Leggette, I want you to take every penny of this, put in your pocket this time 'cause you been giving in this . . . , this church, all your tapes and I feel like you should have something for yourself." They all clapped their hands, made it look like he meant, uh . . . actually made it look like he meant good.

Then I went to church an' I set up in a place where I had set up his inauguration, an' I had sold so many tapes at that spot. So I set up that next Sunday in the spot where I had set up his inauguration; an' I turned the TV on. Now if you don't let the people see at Life Church they wouldn't buy nothing 'cause they would do as the pastor say, but they saw it; Whoo!, they got all excited, an' then uh . . . , that was his inauguration. So, now I was to set up the one I did in Palm Springs, that he said was gonna be mine, an' I was gonna, sell the tapes and give the tapes to the pastor's aid president.

Then what happened when I was on my way inside the church with my equipment, this little deacon came running up to me an' said, "Brother Leggette, the pastor want to see you." And he sounded hastily an' I was trying to see what in the world he want 'cause he done already told me that, uh . . . , I could have it all, so I was disappointed 'cause I wanted to surprise them with giving them the money. So, so . . . here I felt he treated me like I wasn't somebody he knew; he didn't take me in his office and talk to me. Uh . . . , I, uh . . . , I'm a professional person and I felt like that he shoulda did that to me, but he talked in the parking lot. Said . . . , then I walked up to him and I say, "Hey doc, did you want to see me for something, doctor?" He said yes, "We're not showing no tapes today." When he said that, to me that meant . . . , that made me think that he didn't really mean what he had said before at the hotel. So what I did was, I uh . . . , I took . . . , I took my equipment, put it in my car an' I left the church, I didn't change my name from the church roll, I said, well I cain't go along with this, I cain't go along with this.

I was so hurt, the enemy tried to use that to keep me from going to Life Church. So I only stayed there for a little while.

Then I lost my sister; well actually, I had lost my mother, my father; (my father first), my two brothers; then my two sisters. And the last sister (my oldest), I uh . . . , I couldn't hardly make it. So Sister LaVette, one night after my sister passed away, I uh, was taping this lady they called the "Ole Mama", she was marching in acting like the ole Mama an' I got on my knees so I could get a real good shot. When I was on my knees taping it, uh . . . Sister LaVette she . . . , she bowed down, right 'side of me and she said, "Brother Leggette, I heard about the loss of your sister, and you're in our prayers. We're praying for you." That's why I feel today that Sister LaVette is one of the greatest women in the world. She laid hands on me and she prayed while I was trying to make my shots.

So it went on for the funeral service, I kept looking for the pastor to show up, he didn't show up the service, so sister LaVette was there. There's something about these women, brethrens, yeah, it look like God gave them something that we didn't get. So, she came to the funeral and after the funeral was over, I was marched outside the church with the rest of the family an' I was crying. She walked up to me an' she said, "Brother Leggette, I'm praying for you." She said, "God's gonna give you more strength." I looked at her an' I said, "Sister LaVette, I cain't make it, I cain't make it, I-I-I cain't make it now, this is the end of it!" She hit me, knocked me almost down; she said, "You can make it! You've got a wife, you've got kids and you've got sisters and brothers! You can make it!" It felt like a ton of bricks had been lifted off of me. From that point on; I was able to make it.

Pastor J.T. Jones and wife Evang. Mary D. Jones

So later, I was taping in the inauguration service for Pastor
Ron; Pastor J.T. Jones came all the way from . . . Compton and
he came to the inauguration. My wife and I was sitting on two
seats, he squeezed in between us and made three seats outta two.
And he sat between us and He said, "Brother Leggette, How you
doin'?" I said, "I'm okay." He said; (I was crying so I could hardly
see.) He said, "Brother Leggette, I'm praying for you." I said, "You
just came out here to see how I was doing, right?" He said "Yeah,
that's right." He said, "I tell you what I'm gonna do, I'm gonna put
you back on the books. You can go on to Life Church if you want
to, but I'm gonna keep you on the books. So I'm not gonna let you
leave Life Church like this, leave New Jerusalem like this. I want
you to stay with our church so we can see after you, then we can
show you some love."

Pastor William Atlas and Wife, Mary Atlas

So I went on back to his church, I didn't join up, I just went there an' I fellowshipped. Actually I belong to four churches, I belong to New Jerusalem, where Elder William Atlas is Pastor, I belong to Life Church, where Bishop Ron M. Gibson is pastor, I belong to Greater New Jerusalem, where Elder Pearce is the pastor and I belong to Elder Ash's church, Light of the World. So I came out here and that's where I am now. Everybody tell me, you belong to three churches but actually I feel that I belong to four churches.

So I uh . . . I didn't change nothing, my sister . . . , (I lost my health), my little sister, the one that led me to the Lord, I had decided to . . . ; I said "Well, I'm gonna work with my sister now 'cause this is what Daddy and Mother would want. They'd want us to work together as family." An' I started working with my sister as, as uh . . . , uh . . . , I was under watch care; an' I was working with her under watch care. Uh . . . , I go to my sister's church in the daytime and I go to Life Church at night, because that's more convenient for me getting in and out 'cause Life Church got so many people I cain't get in and out that good. So, that's where I am with this Church of God in Christ.

Actually I am Pentecostal from my heart, I was born . . . , I was born in the Church of God in Christ Pentecostal. Then the Lord has certainly been blessing me in a marvelous way, an' I want everybody to know; the only way to go, the only way to go is Pentecostal way, to be saved. The Word; the reason I say Pentecostal, that mean that "on the day of Pentecost they was all with one accord in one place and suddenly there came a sound from heaven as of a rushing mighty wind and it sat upon each of them an' they were filled with the Holy Ghost an' they began to speak with other tongues as the spirit gave them utterance, and they all was filled with the Holy Ghost.

Now the reason the Holy Ghost came, I'm not leaving the subject, the reason the Holy Ghost came, man disobeyed God so much so 'til God repented himself that he made man. That he shut up heaven for a period of four hundred years and He wouldn't hear man pray. So what happened, then God got to thinking 'bout it that, He is so merciful an' such a good God and He thought about it, well I made man for my glory an' I want to bring man back. He said, I tell you what I'ma do; I'm gonna see if I can find somebody that was able to go down and redeem man back. So wh . . . , He searched the heaven, He couldn't find nobody; He searched the earth, He couldn't find nobody; searched beneath the earth, He couldn't find nobody; so the Holy Spirit said, if you prepare me a body I will go down and I'll bring man back. So through a virgin, Mary, He prepared a body an' I say, this is my words, He threw the Holy Ghost down from heaven an' it fell into a virgin girl's womb an' then she become impregnated and then she brought forth her first born son, then after she brought forth Jesus, they killed Him, they hung Him on the cross and then He, He stayed in the grave for three days, then He rose up, when He rose up with all power in His hands, then He decided He would leave the brethren an' go back to heaven with His father. An' He said to the brethren, "I'm gonna leave you, but I'm not gonna leave you comfortless . . . , comfortless, I'm gonna pray to the Father that He would send you another Comforter and He will lead you and guide you and direct you in all the way of truth." Then He was leaving . . . , He was leaving and as He was going up; He was getting higher and higher and higher and higher and the brethren was standing there looking at Him an' they was all excited because He was leaving an' they was sad too! Then while they was looking, He got completely out of sight. Then two men appeared to them in white apparel and they said, "Why ye standing here gazing up in towards the heaven," they say, "the same manner you see Him go He will come in like manner. He will come back after His church without a spot or wrinkle."

So now, if you don't have that Holy Ghost, that's why it's so important; out of this story, this is the most important part of the story of you getting saved and gettin' the Holy Ghost so you be able to go back with the Lord when He comes. He's coming back again because He said, "Behold I come quickly and my reward will be with me to pay every man according to his works." So now, if we don't do what we supposed to do and then we find out at the last minute that we haven't got ourselves ready for the kingdom, . . . then I want let you, . . . I want put this in this story today. Uh . . . Hell is too hot; eternity is too long, for you to find out that you just made a mistake. What I want you to do is, make sure you speak to the Lord now 'cause you got, you got time, you got time now, but tomorrow, tomorrow ain't promised. Since tomorrow's not promised to us, let's just do it now, let's get the Lord in us now 'cause we, 'cause we don't want be caught up in that burning hell forever. Now they tell me that Hell is gonna last forever; say there's no ending and you'll be tormented in the flames forever. And I would like to let all you know that I am Pentecostal and I mean . . . , I don't know how long I'm gonna be living but I mean to be with the Lord until He comes. Thank you all so much for listening to my story an' well . . . , if you don't get nothing else out of this story, I want you to get saved. Get . . . , go to the Lord, all you gotta do is go to Him and repent. The word repent; give up everything that's not like Him and then meet the Lord when He come in the air.

Pastor Ron M. and Lady LaVette Gibson

Well, I'd like to, uh; beginning again with Pastor Ron and the rest of this story. All righty, This is yours truly, Bro Roosevelt Leggette,

I'm grateful to finish up my book. I'd like to record one of the most important and one of the greatest men that ever walked through America. The Lord blessed this Church of God in Christ to have a legacy by the name of Pastor Ron M Gibson. Pastor Gibson married his wife Sis LaVette, then he decided to do something for the Lord. So what he did was, he moved to the Inland Empire and devoted all his time in the gospel, full time. He started a work right there on Rubidoux Boulevard. He moved out here and started 'round a cow pasture in the desert, where nothing was there but horses, ground squirrels, skunks, birds . . . but this man turned this thing into a ministry. He came out here and started a church twenty-three years ago. And right now he started out with nine people, and he's up now to about four thousand or more. Pastor Ron has gone all over the world on Christian television. I went down with him several times an' he went on TBN, went all through Africa and all over America preaching the gospel. He's one man that like to have all the people in the world saved but you . . . , it's kinda hard for you to tell him that he cannot save the all people cause he have . . . , he has a mind to save all colors, Black, White, Mexican, Japanese, Chinese and African; everybody. He goes out for the whole world.

This man built this church, he started out in a li'l old small church then right up the hill from that little church, he built a nice . . . uh, church, it would hold at least about seven or eight hundred. He started out with one service a day in the small church and went from that one service to three services in the big church and have a Sunday night service, and a Wednesday day and a Wednesday night Bible study and the church is full. Now most of the pastors in the region that know him and they see how the Lord has blessed him to grow so fast, they can't understand it themselves, 'cause this little man is moving too fast. He's a good looking li'l ole guy and so he loves the Lord and he loves all the people of God, he encourages everybody to stay with the Lord, and if you're not with the Lord, get saved. I was at his church a number of times and I saw people by the score receiving the gift of the Holy Ghost, getting saved and receiving the Holy Ghost, right there in our eyes just like it happened in the Bible days. Not only is he getting the people saved and filled with the Holy Ghost. The Lord has moved on him and now this man has bought a whole city and he's having it developed and within it he's building a five thousand seat church and it's going to cost about forty to fifty million dollars. He said, "It shall come to pass", "Teamwork makes the dream work". He got a slogan that says, "We are better together."

An' I was 'round with him in his ministry listening to his prosperity ministry and that's where I got . . . , I got debt free, by listening to Pastor Ron's prosperity ministry. He is so powerful, he believes he can ask God for anything and God will do it. So far this man is one of the most blessed pastors that I ever saw in my life. He's got everything he needs and then some, big houses and big cars, money in the bank and he will just give his money away. He goes to TBN, he give them thousands of dollars and he go to . . . , to anybody's church around and then he will give them a great amount of money to help out; then he goes to Memphis, TN for the great Holy Convocation and he gives thousands of dollars, he goes to West Angeles and he gives thousands. Now all of you that want a real good church home and really wanna follow a man that's going somewhere and don't be jealous like the rest of these folks; catch on to the same blessing plan that Pastor Ron follows, and I will assure you that God will bless you. That's where I got a chance to become debt free by following this great man of God. I'm not rich like him yet, but I'm hanging right in there and I wanna be like him one day. I love the Lord, and it says, "Mark the perfect man."

And preachers, bishops, superintendents, if you want your work to grow, and want it to really be something worthwhile, you follow this great man of God. I mean; it ain't no harm in following him. Don't hate him, stop hating on him; start loving on him and God will bless your church, He will bless you just like He blessed Pastor Ron. The favor of God is with Pastor Ron Gibson; he is really blessed!! I remember when he first came and started preaching in this Church of God in Christ; preaching the gospel, nothing but the gospel and God blessed this great man in ministry and folks were getting blessed all over the city, from Compton, to Riverside and Los Angeles all down through there and right now he has made a mark all over the world. He goes everywhere preaching the gospel and he don't, uh . . . whether you like it or not he just tell you like it is, he's a man that's not afraid to preach it like it is. I mean, lotta preachers sugarcoat it, but he don't shu . . . , he doesn't sugarcoat it, he preach it just like it is and that's why I, . . . I follow him because he's doing things that will help folks out in this present world.

He's getting everybody rapture ready; whether you believe it or not the gospel is right by itself, if you don't believe it's right, just keep on living like you living, then you'll wake up in a place, if you're not saved; that you really don't want to be; but if you want to go back with the Lord when he comes, follow this great man of God. That's why I wanted him in my book, I know my book will be successful if I have a man like this from the Church of God in Christ, from the Pentecostal movement leading me all the way. If I'ma . . . If I'm gonna be Pentecostal, I might as well go on and do it all the way, follow the man that is following Christ and, . . and I know I will be successful. My main thing is I want the people to see what happened to me wha' ha', . . . when I came to California; they can look back over my book and see how the Lord brought me through and I was blessed to get hooked up with Pastor Ron Gibson; so right now I know that with his prayers and with his hope and with his power I will go, all . . . , the . . . , way; because I love the Lord that much. An' I'm looking to see the Lord, I'm looking to meet the Lord in following this great man of God. He's not the only man that's right; but he's one of the one's that's right; then all of you that really want to be saved and really wanna go back with the Lord when he comes, PLEASE hook up with this young man of God!

Just because he's got everything look like, just because he's real good looking that don't mean nothing to him, 'cause he pushes all that stuff aside and let the Lord control his life. People are dying by the thousands and they need a savior. They need somebody that . . . , that will not sugarcoat the gospel, that will tell it like it is, like Pastor Ron, tell it like it is, he don't care what happens, how it hurt or how it don't hurt, he just tell the gospel like it is the way the Lord gave it to him. An' I wanna tell you this man has certainly changed the world by his ministry and by,. and by him following the leadership of the Lord. Now, he is in jurisdiction one and the bishop . . . , we got a new bishop now and this new bishop is trying, . . trying to follow the leading of the Lord like the old bishop did. But Pastor Ron has stepped in there and helping him out all he can, along with all the other pastors and superintendents. An' I'm telling you if you expect to get somewhere in this world, you got to follow leadership. Pastor Ron had the following of leadership of the old bishop, so then if you want to go somewhere and wanna go there right like the old bishop was leading us, then stay with Pastor Ron and the new bishop.

I am where I am today because of Pastor Ron Gibson. Everybody tell me that you trying to be like Pastor Gibson, it don't bother me

because the Bible says do what? "Mark the perfect man." If you
wanna go somewhere, get with somebody going somewhere, get on a
ship, launch out in the deep and move and stay with the man of God
and you, . . . it will be a great success. Believe it, believe me.

I wanna tell you something worthwhile, this is one of the greatest
story's that I can tell you about; this great preacher, this great bishop,
this great superintendent, this great administrative assistant. I mean
he is so gifted he's all these things and this prophet, he does it all and
god is really there with him and as long as I live I want to be around
him, they say if you want to be warm get close to the fire.

Sometime when I, . . . I can't see that much now because my sight is
just about gone and I sit on, . . . the sisters let me sit on the front seat.

When I sit on the front seat I have an advantage there 'cause he
walk . . . , he get anointed he walk up and down in front of the pulpit
area, I can discern an see him barely passing by me while I'm sitting on
that seat. When I see that, the anointing of God comes from him, . . .
from me discerning him, into me that's why I like to sit there 'cause
I can feel that anointing. It's good to be close to the fire so you can
feel the warmness of it, that's where it looks like I'm cheating, but I'm
not cheating, I'm getting close where I can be blessed. An' I know he
doesn't mind it, but he probably don't know he got that kinda power
but God empowers people with His power that can help others just
like when the people in the Bible days would walk by the folks and the
their shadow would pass over and they would be healed and blessed.
Pastor Ron has that same kinda power and he is a man of God.

There's a lot of men of God, look like I'm just talking about one
but there are many others. The Bible says give honor to whom honor
is due and give credit to the person that deserve it and this great
man of God deserves all the honor and credit that we can give him.
An' I'm waiting to see that five thousand seat church built and all

them homes, so many hundreds of homes gonna be there for the people. Now look here, listen to this . . . , this man (Pastor Ron) saw Oral Roberts come to his church and release God's anointing on him before he died. Pastor Ron is starting a prayer tower, it's gonna be a twenty-four hour prayer tower you can go upstairs they will have guards around the clock. In this development there will be stores and schools and everything in this facility. If you stay with God and stay with Pastor Ron, you gonna go someplace.

An' I wish the preachers would . . . , it ain't nothing I can do about this, I wish all these preachers would join up with him and put their arms around and hold his arms up and go with the Lord and go all the way to glory other than just hating on him . . . , hating on him. He can't help it cause God is blessing him like that, he's just doing what God told him and that is the result that he's getting. He got a wife that's standing right by his side; very intelligent school teacher; she teaches the new member class and they have twenty-five or thirty people coming out of that new member class. He has more new members graduating getting their certificates than a lot of these churches have in their church, unh . . . whole membership. So; this man must be doing something right, and as long as I live and long as I can move and long as I can . . . , just if I hafta crawl, I wanna go to that church to get my blessing because the blessing of the Lord is in that place. An' I really love being around with him; I yoked up with him about twenty-three years ago when I put . . . , I put the first camera in his church and from that point on God blessed my work.

He blessed my work so I've already built a studio onto my house and I have a wall of fame with all my famous people that I love; I know and all that; I got'em on my wall in my house, my special friends, Pastor Ron's picture on there and many other preachers, pastors and superintendents is on that wall. I did that because I'm in love with the ministry of Pastor Ron M. Gibson. A lot of folk hear this testimony, they might say, "Well, you know, this man talkin' bout this man and you can't make no god out of a man." No I'm not making a god out of him, but I'm just honoring him for who he is! God has blessed him with this gift and the least we can do is hold his arms up like they did in the bible days. As long as they were holding the people's arm up that was in front when they were in leadership they were winning the battle but when they let his arms go down then the battle start getting lost. But we're gonna hold Pastor Ron up; everybody's not gonna hold him up, he got too many haters.

This man here, he understands life in general, sports, you got some people that's so saved they no earthly good, but Pastor Ron's not like that. He love people, young folk, old folk . . . , he give me so much honor when I'm around, he make me feel like; I'm an older man but he make me feel like . . . , that I'm a youngster and I really enjoy being around Pastor Ron M. Gibson, I feel he's one of the greatest that there ever was. And if the Lord bless this book to show any kinda revenue at all, regardless to all them other preachers I wrote about in this book, this ministry would get the top of the line blessing out of the revenue from this book, I'd would like to be able to be one of the one's that help out, help build that forty million dollar church. I'd like to put my stamp on that to say I was a part of that and I hope the Lord will bless me to live to see it finish in process of it. It would be a great, great thing to know that I helped get this beautiful church started, this beautiful city started right here in the beautiful city of Riverside.

I call Pastor Ron Gibson bishop, although I feel the bishop took the bishopship away from him and I was very displeased with it; but God had some more work for him to do; he will be a bishop, he will be a bishop; 'cause right now he's got more people in his church than all the region put together, churches. They have some many churches in this region here, so many churches in jurisdiction one. But, Pastor Ron . . . , when they want some money raised in any kinda movement, uh . . . , they call Pastor Ron, he knows how to do it, he knows how to raise money but they don't want to put him out front and let him be the bishop let him do it like it supposed to be done, like it oughta be done because they have that jealousy in them. Ya' get that jealousy spirit out of you and let the Lord work in your life, things would be even better for all of us.

Now thank you all very kindly and please read my book and do what I asked you to do and I declare you will be blessed. Follow this man of God. He don't beg you for your money 'cause god blessed him for . . . , with everything he need, he don't need . . . , don't hafta' be on nobody's begging list and when you see him walking around, driving around, preaching, he don't look like he's begging you for nothing, 'cause he look like he's the man of God and he's following the leadership of the Lord. God Bless You.!!

Pastor L.C. Ash and Evangelist Olivia Ash

I have seven preachers in all. But this is one of the greatest men we have here in Riverside, California, by the name of Elder Lawrence Charles Ash. He came to California about fifty-two years ago and has made this his home. He is one that has found his course in the ministry and he've gone as far as he could go, he have the baptism of the Holy Ghost and speakin' in tongues as the spirit of God give him utterance. Pastor Ash belongs to this Pentecostal movement and he's right now working with jurisdiction number one under the leadership of our new Bishop J. E. Ealey and the international bishop. He is one that we love, one that we care a lot about, he's a man that loves the people. He moved out here and started a ministry; but before he came out here, he came from Mississippi through Chicago then back to Florida and then out here. He met his wife back there in Mississippi and they got married then started a family and the Lord blessed them with seven beautiful children.

Elder Ash started a work here in Riverside and he was working with many other churches as assistant pastor and now he have his own work. He is the pastor of Light of the World Church of God in Christ. He has been pasturing for about twenty-two or three years and the Lord is adding to the church such as it needed be. Where right now he have quite a few missionaries, he have about twelve or fifteen missionaries that work right along with him along with the general church The Lord has blessed him as he progresses in this spiritual life. He's working with me in every way that he can, I have a disability, I can't see now, when I go places with the region he escorts me into the place and make sure I have a seat, somewhere to sit.

Now we'd like to tell you some of the things about this great man of God. He's a pastor, he's a superintendent and he's working with the finance department an' he's going around helping straighten out some of all these churches that having problems and he's working with the referral committee and he's known to be, throughout all of California, a man of God full of the Holy Ghost. We're grateful to have him working with us.

Pastor Ash loves the family, he's a family man, a church man, he loves everybody. A few years ago we lost our brother and he took out time out of his busy schedule and did a great work for us in this family. So what happened, my brother was living in Cincinnati, Ohio and he got really sick and passed away without having any insurance at all. So we decided that we would like to have the body here in California for a funeral, but his wife at first didn't want to let go the body, she wanted to hold on to it. She wanted to have the funeral back there in Cincinnati, but he had no insurance, so she couldn't have it there because she had no money or insurance, so she released the body to us and I talked with Sister Olivia and Elder Ash and we got the body here by Elder Ash having this expertise, he know how to do things, work through the mortuary. He got the body here and he had a meeting in his church; called all of my brothers and sisters together that one's of us that was left (there are seven of us). Then he was the first man laid down money to help out with this movement, he laid down one thousand dollars, then we had a meeting and we raised enough money to bury my brother in a decent way. He said in the meeting that he would not have my brother cremated, he was going to have a decent burial, he buried . . . , he did everything he could to get him buried here. He funeralized him, he did the eulogy and then he had some people helping him.

I got a chance to talk with Elder Atlas, Elder William Atlas to help with the funeral and he moderated; Elder Willie Pearce was working standing on the side, everything he could do he was there to do it and after we got to the church, we got ready to march in, Elder

Pearce led us in the church an' he did that little talk as we walked in the church. Then after we got inside we had the scripture and prayer and so on; then Elder Atlas took it from there and after he finished that, then he gave it to Elder Ash. Then after Elder Ash finished the preaching of the funeral, then we went to the grave site Elder Pearce did that ceremony and he laid him to rest.

Everybody had a great part in the home going of my brother. I want to let you know that all you that know about the Pentecostal movement, we are a bunch of people that are born of the spirit of God, it just like it happened back in the Bible days, in Acts 2:4, that's the way it is, the way it work with us now. Elder Ash is one of those kinda men that you can depend on wherever you go. If you really want to go and be with the Lord you need to go and join up with Elder Ash and all these other fine preachers and let the Lord bless your soul where you'll be ready to meet Him in that great day when the Lord come back again so you be ready to go. So we thank God, thank God for Pastor Ash and the Light of the World Church for sharing with us with everything he got, he's a great man of God who we love and we really, we really appreciate this great man of god. Thank you all very much for letting me write about this great man. Now everyone listen and read about him and find out who he is, 'cause he came from a beautiful family; Bishop Hughes which is his uncle; then he knows everything about this Church of God in Christ and he knows how to get you there.